SOURCES AND TRAJECTORIES

Sources *and* Trajectories

Eight Early Articles
by Jacques Ellul
That Set the Stage

Translation and Commentary by

MARVA J. DAWN

WILLIAM B. EERDMANS PUBLISHING COMPANY
GRAND RAPIDS, MICHIGAN / CAMBRIDGE, U.K.

© 1997 Wm. B. Eerdmans Publishing Co.
255 Jefferson Ave. S.E., Grand Rapids, Michigan 49503 /
P.O. Box 163, Cambridge CB3 9PU U.K.
All rights reserved

Printed in the United States of America

02 01 00 99 98 97   7 6 5 4 3 2 1

Library of Congress Cataloging-in-Publication Data

Ellul, Jacques.
Sources and trajectories: eight early articles / by Jacques Ellul;
translation and commentary by Marva J. Dawn.
        p.   cm.
ISBN 0-8028-4268-2 (pbk.: alk. paper)
1. Theology. 2. Sociology, Christian. 3. Sociology.
I. Dawn, Marva J. II. Title.
BR85.E489 1997
230'.42 — dc21   96-37693
                                        CIP

In Memory of Jacques Ellul, 1912-1994

Prophet, Social Critic, Scholar
Bible Study Leader and Preacher
Nurturer of Young People
Professor, Adviser, Writer
Resister, Farmer, Environmental Activist
Model, Mentor, Sage
Admonisher, Questioner, Sufferer
Friend to Many
Faithful to Vocation and Revelation

Contents

Contents

Introduction

What a great loss it was to the world when, on May 19, 1994, French sociologist and lay theologian Jacques Ellul died! Those of us who were stirred by Ellul to new levels of questioning and new modes of thinking (the last thing he wanted was "disciples") believe that his gifts to the world have not received adequate attention. Perhaps this book can counteract that inadequacy a little by introducing new readers to some of his key ideas and by connecting his previous readers to some of the roots of his work.

Dr. Steven Hubble, professor of ecology at Princeton University, spoke recently on National Public Radio about the need for a broad view so that problems do not slip through the cracks of various specializations.[1] Our culture is desperate for "Renaissance people" who can give such expansive perspectives. One person who bequeathed such perspectives was Jacques Ellul.

This book is composed of eight articles written by Ellul and not previously translated into English. The eight were chosen not necessarily for their clarity or power to convince, but because they are the earliest formulations of some of Ellul's key ideas. We see in them the roots of, and foundational agenda for, the work of the mature

---

1. Dr. Hubble is also chair of the Committee for a National Institute of the Environment. His NPR comments on November 17, 1995, used the example that we know about the ozone hole, but we do not know how it affects such things as fishing. Ellul would certainly have supported an endeavor for composite ecological thinking.

1

Ellul. My introductory "Source" comments in each chapter will give background material for placing the article in the context of Ellul's life, while the "Trajectory" comments will illustrate how the main ideas of the article were expanded or more clearly formulated in Ellul's later works.

It is important to emphasize that these are articles by the *young* Jacques Ellul, so they are often impetuous, driving, inconsistent. Sometimes his usual foibles (see below) are even more exaggerated. But these essays also reveal his brilliance and immense insight. Ellul always continued to study, to refine, and to gather a vast wealth of information as background to future books. Ivan Illich, in a speech at the symposium held in Ellul's honor at the University of Bordeaux in November 1993, praised him as follows:

> After spending a few evenings immersed in this treasure [of about twenty of Ellul's books], I was astounded by the freshness and vivacity with which, over the years, Ellul continually recaptures the fundamental intuitions of his earliest work, always clarifying them more. His tenacity, humility and magnanimity in the face of criticism make him an example one must bow to.
>
> The present scholarly meeting at Bordeaux furnishes us with a unique opportunity to acknowledge the unity of his thought. Some of us have read him as a great commentator on the Bible, others, as a philosopher of technology. But few have seen him as the man who simultaneously challenges the reflection of both the philosopher and the believer. He reminds the philosopher of technology, who studies patent, observable phenomena, to be aware of the possibility that his subject may be too terrible to be grasped by reason alone. And he leads the believer to deepen his Biblical faith and eschatological hope in the face of two uncomfortable and disturbing truths . . . [that of] modern technique and its malevolent consequences [and that of the] subversion of the Gospel — its transformation into an ideology called Christianity.[2]

The essays in this book are some of Ellul's first written statements of those "fundamental intuitions." They will reveal both sides

---

2. Ivan Illich, "An Address to 'Master Jacques,' " *The Ellul Forum* 13 (July 1994): 16.

2

of Ellul's work and the ways in which, at the beginning, he tied them together.

Ellul's Place in the Spectrum of the Disciplines: Social Theory, Biblical Hermeneutics, Ethics

Ellul first became well known in the United States in 1964 when *The Technological Society* was translated into English (ten years after its initial appearance in France) and introduced by Robert Merton, professor of sociology at Columbia University. Two important sequels to this work were *The Technological System* (1977/80)[3] and *The Technological Bluff* (1988/90), but before these two he had published books about propaganda (1962/65), political illusions (1965/67), cliches (*A Critique of the New Commonplaces* — 1966/68), revolutions (1969/71), violence (published in English first, 1969), and modern forms of the sacred (*The New Demons* — 1973/75). These works, which philosophize about large moral issues and deal centrally with the problem of power, are named *sociologie* in Europe, but would be better labeled in the United States as "critical social thought." Ellul also wrote literally hundreds of articles detailing various observations about the technological society.

Though Ellul might be considered one example of a particularly eminent line of social theorists (including such people as Marcuse and Durkheim), he goes against the tide in the field of biblical hermeneutics. His criticism of some modern methods of biblical exegesis is severe, and sometimes his own methods seem to lack essential rigor. His biblical works include volumes on Jonah (1952/71), II Kings (*The Politics of God and the Politics of Man* — 1966/72), Revelation (1975/77), and Ecclesiastes (1989/90) and treatments of the subjects of money (*Money and Power* — 1954/85) and the city (*The Meaning of the City* — in English first, 1970).

In the field of ethics, the influence of both Kierkegaard and Barth is evident. Rather than outlining a system of ethics along

---

3. Throughout this book the dates for Ellul's works will list the year of publication in French first, followed by the English year of publication.

the classical deontological (rules-based) or teleological (goals-based) lines, Ellul posits an *Ethics of Freedom* (1973/76), which is radically Christocentric and practically applied to such issues as the use of money (1954/85), the practice of prayer (*Prayer and Modern Man* — in English first, 1970), and the way our culture destroys language by misuse and by its emphasis on the visual (*The Humiliation of the Word* — 1981/86).

We will see the roots of this wide range of subjects in the eight articles that follow. More important, we will see how the subjects are connected, and — in this postmodern world grasping for perspective and reference points — we will discover ways in which Ellul's worldview can guide us.

Avoiding Misunderstandings Generated by Problems in Ellul's Style

Undoubtedly, Ellul's writings frustrate his readers in many ways. He frequently overstated his case in order to make a point or misrepresented particular elements of the landscape in his attempt to paint the whole scene with broad brushstrokes. One of the most difficult barriers is the fact that he worked in two completely separate tracks — theology and *sociologie* — and rarely connected the two (*The Humiliation of the Word* is a major exception), so readers who didn't know the larger corpus would think that his social analyses were vastly overstated pessimism or that his theological reflections were idealistically naive optimism. Ellul himself said at the symposium in his honor,

> I have always tried to prevent "my" theology from influencing my sociological research (Calvinism) and my comprehension of the world from distorting my reading of the Bible. These were two domains, two methods, two distinct interests. Only after the separation, one begins to perceive relationship.[4]

4. Jacques Ellul, "Ellul's Response to the Symposium in His Honor at the University of Bordeaux, November 1993," trans. Achim Koddermann and Carl Mitcham, *The Ellul Forum* 13 (July 1994): 18.

The eight articles contained in this volume will lay some groundwork so that readers can see the dialectical connections between Ellul's two tracks, recognize his foibles and impetuosity, discover the trajectory of Ellul's life project, and experience the brilliance of his perceptions. It is my hope that these excerpts will enable readers unfamiliar with Ellul to find some starting points into his immense corpus of stimulating work.

Another difficulty in encountering Ellul lies in his quirky disavowal of systems. This rejection does not mean that Ellul is simply contradictory or incoherent, for, indeed, there is a deep coherence in all that he writes. He believed, however, that systematic formulations cannot deal with the dialectical nature of reality, that apparent "contradictions" in actuality demonstrate that a message is too large for our categories. Ellul intended, therefore, that his work confront critical social analysis dialectically with theological and biblical knowledge without "any artificial or philosophical synthesis." Ellul refused "to construct a *system* of thought, or to offer up some Christian or prefabricated socio-political solutions." Instead, he wanted "to provide Christians with the means of thinking out *for themselves* the meaning of their involvement in the modern world." Ellul said it was not possible for him to look at anything *sub specie aeternitatis* because everything he thought, did, and wrote as a Christian was done in relation to a specific setting. External events and sociological, political, and ideological permutations, therefore, are highly influential because he thought "at grips" with his surroundings.[5]

This does not mean, however, that his work merely conformed to the changing currents of the times. Rather, Ellul's approach permitted him to refrain from being mentally "committed" to any particular school of thought or to any specific program of action. On the other hand, his work was firmly based on the fact that he was "involved" in his relationship with Jesus Christ. The anonymous translator of these words explained in a footnote that Ellul used the word *engagé* (translated "committed") to signify that

5. Jacques Ellul, "From Jacques Ellul . . . ," *Introducing Jacques Ellul*, ed. James Y. Holloway (Grand Rapids: William B. Eerdmans, 1970), p. 6; emphasis Ellul's.

which he rejected because the word carried clearly ideological political connotations in France and because he refused to pledge his mind to "anything or anyone, save Jesus Christ."[6]

Chapter Contents

Ellul's "involvement" with Jesus Christ is evident in all the articles in this book. Though later in life he rarely mixed his *sociologie* with his Christian faith, "Political Realism" (Article 3 in this volume; 1947), the third article in a series in *Foi et Vie* (Faith and Life), is two-thirds a critique of political realism and one-third a delineation of Christian realism as the only true alternative. The way was prepared for this analysis of false and true realism by the first two articles in the *Foi et Vie* series. The first, "Chronicle of the Problems of Civilization" (Article 1; 1946), criticizes false utopias and suggests instead that the basic structures of society must be understood. The second, "Needed: A New Karl Marx" (Article 2; 1947), describes the kind of thorough investigation that is required. That article ends with an inventory of the structures to be considered, of which politics is the first.

Both the fourth and the seventh articles in this volume elaborate and model for us the Christian realism introduced earlier in # 3. Article 4, "On Christian Pessimism" (1954), demonstrates that genuine Christianity is neither pessimism nor optimism; article 7, "Christian Faith and Social Reality" (1960), is the only example of Ellul's speeches included in this book.

Article 5, "The Meaning of Freedom According to Saint Paul" (1951), provides the biblical basis for Ellul's major work in ethics, *The Ethics of Freedom*. The remaining two articles, # 6 and # 8, are included here not because they are so early but because they emphasize ideas not found in this fashion elsewhere, though much of Ellul's work is built on their conclusions. Article 6, "The Contemporaneity of the Reformation" (1959), challenges present-day Christians to imitate not the specific content but the attitudes and

---

6. Jacques Ellul, "Mirror of These Ten Years," *Christian Century* 87, 7 (Feb. 18, 1970): 200.

faithfulness of the sixteenth-century Reformers. It thereby gives us a description of what Ellul himself was trying to do in his theological work, much as the "Karl Marx" article (Article 2) shows us what he was doing in his *sociologie*.

The final article (# 8), "Innocent Notes on 'The Hermeneutical Question'" (1968), gives us a glimpse into the perspectives that underlie Ellul's specifically biblical works. Since the latter go against the tide of much of modern biblical criticism, it is an extremely important piece for understanding both Ellul's contributions to theological discussion and the antagonisms that he raised.

Procedures for Translation

I must emphasize that I undertook this project, not because I have the skills or expertise to produce this book, but because my dissertation work made very clear its necessity. The endeavor would have been impossible without John H. Yoder's foundational help with the first reading of the French texts. In addition, his comment about the need for further study on Ellul and the Powers invited me to adopt this subject for my doctoral research, and he served as the dissertation director at the University of Notre Dame. John's deep familiarity with Ellul's context through his own work in Europe after World War II filled in many informational gaps.

Three other persons provided significant expertise for this project. Without Joyce Main Hanks's thoroughly extensive bibliographical work, I never would have discovered these articles in the first place. Dr. Neal Blough, director of the "Centre Mennonite d'Etudes et de Rencontre" (the Mennonite Center for Study and Fellowship) in Paris, gave me both translation and context help. I met Neal when he came to the U.S. for a year and taught a course on Ellul at the Associated Mennonite Biblical Seminary in Elkhart, Indiana; he and his wife Jan hosted me graciously in Paris when I went to France to interview Ellul. Neal's assistance came from a deep acquaintance with Ellul's ideas, and he provided invaluable contributions for understanding their setting.

Neal's friend, Pastor Bernard Charles, a retired French Reformed pastor, who knew Ellul personally and lived through the period in which the following articles were written, provided comments as well as photocopies of related articles from French journals to clarify elements of the context. For many years Pastor Charles has read *Foi et Vie* (the journal from which many of these articles are taken and of which Ellul became editor in 1969) and has been actively involved in the French Fellowship of Reconciliation and "Christianisme social" (to which Ellul refers), so the information he provided helped immensely to put these articles in their proper context.

I must add, however, that even with the help of the above-named scholars and two local French professors I was unable to track down some of Ellul's references. As Dr. Blough noted in a letter, "Ellul's writing is difficult to translate because he makes so many allusions to people, places, events, theories that are not always obvious even to the French reader." Moreover, even though we might ascertain the specifics of Ellul's notations, we still might not understand what Ellul meant by it. On one question Dr. Blough consulted a French friend who is a brilliant sociologist and knows Ellul's works well, but even he could not understand what Ellul meant. I regret that Ellul is not still alive to ask him questions.

The persons listed above are not responsible for the final shape that my translations and annotations took, but I owe them immense gratitude for their gifts of knowledge and time. I apologize to the reader for gaps that remain and hope that confusions are due to Ellul's sometimes less-than-careful writing and not to weaknesses in my own attempts to translate faithfully.

I took my main cues for translating from Robert Alter, biblical translator and teacher of Hebrew and comparative literature at the University of California in Berkeley. Alter criticizes "dynamic equivalent" renderings because such translations tend to heighten the language of the original. His work led me to a conscious decision to be true to Ellul's vocabulary — copying his insistent repetition of primary terms, but choosing an unusual word when he did without amplifying his vocabulary.

Throughout, it took great effort to resist the temptation to fix Ellul's style. I have refrained from eliminating extra connecting words, making passive verbs active, turning fragments into whole sentences, separating run-ons, etc., in order to preserve the style of the early Ellul. I have followed Ellul's inconsistencies in capitalization, except where it was necessary to capitalize some names for God, like "Wholly Other," to avoid confusion and where English practice requires capitalizing names of denominations and adjectives of national names. A few times I have also capitalized entire connecting words to aid the reader in following Ellul's argument.

Punctuation often had to be changed to follow English rules a bit more closely or to eliminate confusion or to set off misplaced modifiers, but I have tried to keep Ellul's run-on style whenever reasonably possible so that readers can catch his impetuosity as one thought immediately piles into the next. I have also singularized his editorial *we* to make more clear specific references to himself.

The one main exception to the rule of close imitation was to turn Ellul's constant use of "l'homme" or "man" into inclusive language, except in one instance where his sense would have been lost (see Chapter 3, p. 80). Because of Ellul's emphasis on the person, his abhorrence of violence, and his very great kindness to visitors (myself included), I think he would be using inclusive language by now, though his resistance to cultural fads would prevent him from some of the follies to which political correctness sometimes leads.

Except where specifically stated, the footnotes in each article are not Ellul's, but contain information added by me and most often given by the helpers noted above or gleaned from various biographical and historical resources. Translations of quotations from other previously untranslated Ellul works besides these eight articles are also mine.

Since some of my own books don't include introductions with acknowledgments, this one gives me the chance to thank Jennifer Hoffman, my editor at Eerdmans, who always does a superb job. Jennifer's graciousness in preserving my style and vocabulary helped me to realize that I should try to do the same for Ellul.

CHAPTER 1

"Chronicle of the Problems of Civilization"

SOURCES

Published in 1946, this is one of Ellul's first major articles. Joyce Main Hanks's comprehensive bibliography lists only a few articles, including two longer ones on law and on fascism, written before 1945, and in that year several short editorial pieces for *Réforme,* dealing with communism, capitalism, Hitler, and the war.[1] In this article, the first of three in a series in *Foi et Vie,* Ellul critiques much of the response to the end of World War II and introduces his notion of the structures of society.

One of the main problems in Ellul's style (which a translator should not tamper with) shows up glaringly in this article — that of overstatement. The difficulty makes us ask, however, what it means for us at the end of the twentieth century if Ellul said in 1946 that the world was about to fall apart. Does it signify that the problem has been solved and humanity has survived — or does it mean that being about to collapse is a permanent condition? David Neville, coeditor of the Australian Baptist Peace Fellowship's journal, *Faith and Freedom,* wisely uses this self-description of writer Flannery O'Connor to explain Ellul's overstatements:

---

1. Joyce Main Hanks, compiler, with the assistance of Rolf Asal, "Jacques Ellul: A Comprehensive Bibliography," in *Research in Philosophy and Technology* (London: Jai Press, 1984), pp. 4-5.

When you assume that your audience holds the same beliefs you do, you can relax a little and use more normal means of talking to it; when you have to assume that it does not, then you have to make your vision apparent by shock — to the hard of hearing you shout, and for the almost-blind you draw large and startling figures. . . . Those writers who speak for and with their age are able to do so with a great deal more ease and grace than those who speak counter to prevailing attitudes.[2]

Much of Ellul's work proceeds from insights opposed to general persuasions and is intended to wake his readers up. In many cases in these articles we will find that Ellul's warnings are even more desperately needed now than when he first wrote them. As he would say, the prophetic work is never finished, but must always be done afresh in each generation.

At two places in the following text Ellul refers to himself as a historian, which must be understood from Ellul's own comments. He studied law because his father demanded it, but he was not interested in any of its professions. He "developed a love for Roman law because of its imperturbable logic" and because he had loved history since high school.[3] Ellul's doctoral dissertation (1936) was a "Study of the Evolution and Juridical Nature of *Mancipium*," a Roman institution that allowed a father to sell his son. In 1943 he received the "agrégation" in law, which permitted him to teach on the basis of a competitive examination for only a very few university posts and his book-length manuscript, "Introduction to the History of the Discipline of Reformed Churches in France." From 1943 to 1980 he taught courses in Roman law and the history and sociology of institutions at the University of Bordeaux and at the Institute of Political Studies in Bordeaux (1947-1980). During that time he produced five volumes in

2. Flannery O'Connor, *Mystery and Manners,* ed. Sally Fitzgerald and Robert Fitzgerald (New York: Farrar, Straus & Giroux, 1961), pp. 34 and 47, quoted in David Neville, "Confronted with New Perspectives: Reading Jacques Ellul," *Faith and Freedom* 3, 4 (December 1994): 25.

3. Jacques Ellul, *In Season, Out of Season: An Introduction to the Thought of Jacques Ellul,* based on interviews by Madeleine Garrigou-Lagrange, trans. Lani K. Niles (San Francisco: Harper & Row, 1982), p. 21. Most of the biographical information in this introduction is taken from this book.

Histoire des institutions (the History of Institutions, never translated into English).

However, Ellul did not write about civilization from an ivory-tower perspective. Having received the Doctor of Law degree from the University of Bordeaux in 1936, he taught law for a year in Montpellier, participated briefly in the Spanish Civil War in 1937, was transferred to Strasbourg in 1938, and was moved with the rest of the school to Clermont-Ferrand in 1939 because of World War II. When he was discharged in 1940 because a student reported his opposition to the Vichy government and it was discovered that his father was a foreigner, Jacques and his wife Yvette supported their family (two of their four children were born before he returned to teaching) by farming at Martres (about forty kilometers from Bordeaux), where they actively participated in the Resistance movement by hiding Jews. At war's end, Jacques was appointed to the liberation city council at Bordeaux and served as deputy mayor in the areas of commerce and public works. During the year and a half that he served on the council, Ellul learned, as he says, "what little room for action a politician has."[4] Dissatisfied by his experiences in this post, he quit politics in 1947. The following article was written in the midst of this disillusioning involvement.

4. Ellul, *In Season,* p. 53.

12

Chronicle of the Problems of Civilization
1. By Way of a Brief Preface

Jacques Ellul

The current epoch is productive of problems. Yet both intellectuals and the everyday person are singularly slow to take stock of their conditions — to say nothing of seeking solutions. These problems are born of factual circumstances, of the development of techniques or of the economy, of social developments (sociological or psychological), of spiritual and artistic developments — and all these are presently changing rapidly. Often the problems have been modified before we have even become aware of their existence. It is quite ridiculous, for example, after the war we have experienced, to observe politicians using a form of diplomacy and methods of world organization, the principles of which go back to 1648.[1]

Our contemporaries are obsessed by certain images of "the questions" (e.g., the social question, the communist question, the German question, the planned economy question, etc.). With the patience of an ant tirelessly dragging a cricket's wing, with the incoherence of ants all harnessed to the same task and each tugging in a different direction, we insist obstinately on resolving these "questions" as if they were contemporary. And we struggle, and we fight for such a solution, as if it had the least real importance, without seeing that the social question is practically resolved, that

1. The date 1648 signifies the Order of Westphalia. That treaty at the end of the "Thirty Years' War" is taken as laying the foundation of a world made up of "nations," each claiming "sovereignty."

"Chronique des Problèmes de Civilisation I: En Guise d'Avertissement," *Foi et Vie* 44, 6 (September/October 1946): 678-87.

the German question was posed in 1870, that communism has won the game in human terms and in a yet undefined form, etc.[2] It is a matter of a constant battle with shadows that fade away as soon as we think we have grasped them.

There are two reasons for this [tendency to concentrate on obsolete questions]. The first is that we tie ourselves to exterior forms without searching for their deeper reality. We want to combat social injustice, and that is very good, and we connect it to an economic system, but we do not penetrate the true structures of this system. We do not attempt to penetrate into the lair of the blacksmith who is forging our chains, whether because of a sacred fear of this mystery or because of an incapacity to go far enough. It is easier to accuse two hundred families, the Jews, or the bolshevik with a knife between his teeth — beyond that, we seem to have no way to get a hold on things. Nevertheless, it is only by going beyond that [into more critical analysis] that we will have any chance of encountering the more stable reality on which the shifting problems depend. It is in such a descent into hell[3] that we might be able to grasp the element of continuity according to which the current difficulties are propelled. It is in attacking these roots that we have a chance of reaching the tree itself, and not in the chasing of leaves blown by the hazards of the wind.

The other [reason that we tend to concentrate on obsolete questions] is that we consider our civilization quite stable and quite satisfactory, even if, and especially if, we protest against

2. Ellul means that the German problem is much older, that it goes back at least to 1870, and therefore is not a contemporary one. Handling the German question differently in 1870 might have led to a situation different from World War II, which ended the year before this article was written. We will see later in the essay that Ellul refers to communism, not as incarnated in the form of the Soviet empire, but in the theoretical terms of the socialist ideal. Ellul comments below on how socialist thought had largely won the allegiance of the intellectuals of his time and place.

3. Ellul uses the phrase *descente aux enfers* here, which is the technical term referring to the credal affirmation of Christ's triumphant descent to hell. Having extensively studied Ellul's use of the concept of the "principalities and power," I am convinced that he is noting here the necessity for understanding the evil powers, over which Christ triumphed on the cross, as sources of problems in the world.

14

iniquity, inequality, slavery, etc.; in other words, within this normal healthy body there are wounds that mar its beauty. In this progress toward well-being and being better still, there are hitches that make us lose ground. And we carry with us our Band-Aids to heal the wounds and our motors to get us going again. Communism, nuclear fission, the Beveridge plan,[4] the United Nations — all these are, on the same level, examples of Band-Aids. Now, what we do not see is that much more than that is at stake today. At stake is a problem of civilization that can be posed very simply thus: EITHER our civilization will continue on these same foundations, with its same dominant ideas, the same basic structures, and then humankind will die — spiritually and perhaps also materially.

OR rather life will triumph within humankind, and then civilization will change its foundations and its structures. We are at an absolutely decisive point — such as there has never been before. And it is as a historian that I write that sentence — that is, as a person who knows how psychosis magnifies the present facts in a monstrous way, who knows what their contemporaries thought of Attila or of Tamerlane, who knows what the year 1000 was.[5] I hope later to justify this claim that our time is incommensurable with the rest of history and that the dilemma posed is an authentic one without loophole and without compromise. It is necessary for us, people of 1946, to make a decision about the question of the structures of our society. It is truly the problem of all our civilization

4. William Beveridge was an English lord who wrote a plan on social security in 1942 and one on employment in 1944. These plans were important in the complicated context of the reconstruction of postwar France, the rise of communism in Eastern Europe, and so on. Ellul was extremely well aware of all that was being written in terms of social planning and political philosophy. See note 2 above concerning Ellul's use of the word *communism*.

5. Ellul's point is that, in spite of obsessive magnification of the present conditions, the situation is indeed more critical than when Attila (406[?]-453), the ferocious king of the Huns, earned his name "the Scourge of God," or when Timor the lame (Tamerlane), a Mongol warrior (1336[?]-1405), conquered territory from the Black Sea to the upper Ganges. The idea that the year 1000 was marked by terrific popular terror has dubious historical attestation, but present media and cultural hype about the coming of the year 2000 makes this idea about medieval Europe understandable.

that is posed, of our civilization which is perhaps not far from total collapse.[6]

*　　*　　*

I realize that the reader will say, "more pessimism." However, we have to clarify this pessimism business! For myself I don't know what this pessimism or optimism is; what I do know is that the world in which I live is the domain of Satan, that human beings, myself included, are radically sinful, and that God, miraculously, allows them to live. He organizes a world for them, but all that these sinful people know how to do is to destroy it, and yet indefinitely God maintains it in spite of them. It cannot be otherwise, for human beings separated from God are separated from the source of life. They are doomed to die and can produce only death. But God does more than preserve. He saves. He gives to human beings a path whereby they recover life. He gives to human beings a truth by which they become capable of acting. And God saves in such a way that the prince of this world is subordinated to the salvation of humankind by virtue of the victory of the Savior who becomes Lord. There is no other way, no other truth, that could allow us to act and to live. Outside of that, there is only death. Consequently, whenever I see a human effort in another direction — when I see a human construction that does not take account of the Lord and of the order established by God — I know inevitably where that has to lead: to ruin and condemnation. There isn't any pessimism in that; it is an observation of the same order as the one I would make in seeing the driver of a car going sixty fall asleep at the wheel: it is not pessimism to say that there are certain physical and mechanical laws according to which unavoidably there will be an accident *under these conditions.* If the [human] order disregards the laws of God's

---

6. Since Ellul wrote this in 1946, we have to ask what it means for us at the close of the twentieth century. Certainly it is not the case that the problem Ellul identified has been remedied and humankind's survival ensured. Perhaps we can see both that the situation of a collapsing civilization is still — and much more so — the case and also that Ellul, as he often does, overstates his theme to make his point.

order, and fails to recognize the meaning of the entire work of God turned toward the Cross, it is not any pessimism to observe that the civilization built by this humankind is going toward death. But this situation is included within a parenthesis; it is encompassed somehow within the vaster fact of the Lordship of Jesus Christ and the work of salvation. In other words, *such* a human work is bound to fail, but that does not mean that human beings are condemned for this and that the life of the world because of this is radically jeopardized — for the victory has been definitively won, death is already vanquished, the work of God is already accomplished. Thus these successive human failures can change nothing in the cosmic situation, any more than in the situation of human beings before God. Whether a person succeeds in some material creation or fails miserably, that makes no difference in the condition of the sinful person. The person is nonetheless saved by Jesus Christ. And this is no more optimism than what [I was saying] a moment ago was pessimism. I am not optimistic about the French army when I affirm that Philippe Auguste won the battle of Bouvines.[7] This is a reality that is continuously true. It is no different from what is expressed by my affirmation, "Jesus Christ vanquished Satan" or "Jesus Christ is risen" — therefore humankind in its present reality can be saved. Thus in this study there is neither pessimism nor optimism. There is here a realistic examination of the factual situation, a situation that is one moment of the action of God on the earth and that we must consequently never cease to consider as being on the line that runs from the Resurrection to the Parousia.

*   *   *

Would I then say, "I take no further interest, then, in the fate of this civilization"? No doubt yes, if I were pure spirit. Yes again, if I had only my own isolated self in view. But here, as with a body given by God, I live in this world amidst people to whom I am to be a neighbor. Thus [it is] impossible for me to retreat to that

7. Philippe Auguste, king of France, defeated a coalition of the German emperor, the count of Flanders, and the king of England at the battle of Bouvines in 1214.

untroubled solution. There is the concern that the people who surround me live a life such that they can hear the words that liberate. There is the concern that the victory of Jesus Christ be experienced in and by these people. There is the concern of the fracas for the world where these people live, that it might be more livable — and thereby conformed to what God wanted for this world. Even in this affair I cannot have the same attitudes and the same judgments as the other people. For I am situated in a perspective that is a bit peculiar. Citizen of two cities, I have in hand a particular instrument that obliges me to examine different facts and [to examine them] differently: the discernment of spirits. I thus cannot be content with the opinion, ill-conceived or profound, that people have concerning their affairs, any more than with the solutions, technical or spiritual, that they work out. Everything must be sifted through the sieve of the factual situation I was describing above, and nothing can spare us this work — whether the world be euphoric or feverish — for, truly, the world cannot do without this work, which consists in seeking out the ultimate roots of the present situation and in judging everyday facts spiritually. Only that can provide intelligible continuity to political and social events.

Now this discovery of a continuity is of such importance that in large part it explains the ascent of Marxism. Until now [our cultural life] was totally incoherent. The churches had renounced their mission in the world. Liberalism was barely capable of taking stock of the superficial connectedness of events without [perceiving] any inner necessity. Marxism applies its method, and everything becomes luminous. Human beings find themselves finally in a world where they can move about knowing from where they come and where they are going. And if existentialism has any political bearing today, it is that of being the living proof of the failure of Marxism. Because the latter is really overwhelmed by events, once again absurdity, incoherence become the adjunct of existence. There is no longer a possible future. There is only a freedom that knocks a person over like a stone into the obscurity of nothingness. Thus becomes evident the necessity of discovering, ever anew, the structures of our world, as something of a bridge between the eternal act of God and the present moment, which we live with the duty to act in this world according to the will of God. It is a matter on the whole of bringing our time into line with what it has been given us to know about the Revelation. Then it is a matter of proceeding to actualize the Gospel as much for the world where we are as for ourselves. Now, this work must ceaselessly be done again. It can never be enclosed in a theological *summa,* nor in a political or economic system; the face of this world changes. We cannot once for all benefit from the lessons of history nor from the good relations established between the Church and the world. [It is] the task of the pioneer, the inventor, for which almost every Christian generation must accept responsibility again, lest the Church prefer to fall asleep in the pleasant contemplation of the promise that the gates of death will not prevail against her. But when she sleeps is she still the Church?

In any case the question seems singularly complicated today — nearly desperate. The complexity of our organizations, the enormous quantity of problems, the frenzy of the economic realm, the Church's long lack of interest, and the despair — the immeasurable despair of people today.[8] All these things, which add up to the eve of the end of a civilization, incite us to the work, with urgency, and at the same time discourage us by its apparent vanity.

Nevertheless, "when the wind rises, one must try to live."[9]

* * *

In the theme that I wish to open up with these remarks, I shall not seek to achieve this work totally. I am attempting simply to make an inventory. Beyond the social and economic forms, there are forces that condition the life of our time. These forces are identical

---

8. Ellul actually says "le désespoir sans nombre des hommes," which literally means "the despair innumerable." One French adviser suggested that "counting" is an odd thing to do with despair(s) and that perhaps Ellul intended "sans nom" or "unnamable." I think instead that Ellul did indeed mean "without number" since in other places he writes about the many kinds of despair in the modern world, so I have used the word *immeasurable* to imply both range and depth.

9. French pastor Bernard Charles recognized that this quotation comes from André Gide and is an allusion to the "wind of liberty" and to the biblical "le vent souffle ou il veut" ("the wind blows where it wills"), a reference to the Holy Spirit (cf. John 3:8).

throughout the world; they are common to all our civilization; they are independent of human will; they have a reality not easily separable from their temporary form; finally, they give to our time its radically new character. It is the inventory of these forces that I shall attempt to make. Therefore, it will be a matter not of exhausting the question nor of providing the solutions. To exhaust the question is neither my object nor my pretension. We are here in a nearly new realm. Each of the points that I shall indicate would merit a scientific study in one or more volumes. Thus it is a matter more of opening the way to the research than of [reaching] any conclusion. To provide solutions is even less possible: before seeking the solution we must find a method; before seeking a method we must pose the problem. Now the course of history has posed the problem perfectly, but it has not yet been reduced to intelligible terms, and consequently we cannot have an adequate method, and still less a solution. For this is the folly of our time: we claim to give solutions without even looking at the problems. We cast a superficial glance over the world and pretend to organize it for a thousand years. It is not one of the least contradictory traits of our epoch that we demand answers before we are capable of formulating clearly the questions. But then, is not the historian obligated to ask the reason for this incapacity?

The fact seems clear enough. We are in an essentially materialist time, or rather, a time of radical separation between two realms, material and spiritual. For economic or political problems, economic or political responses. The separation of the realms prohibits going further, and particularly seeking in this realm spiritual causes and foundations, envisaging all the data of our times from a spiritual perspective, as is essential. And therein we find the common measure [linking] the incoherent phenomena we are watching. It would be, therefore, a matter of Christianity succeeding at getting rid of the iron corset that was imposed on it, in order to resume its research and the analysis of this time. To that end it would be necessary for the Church to be armed with an exact and solid theology and to know how to apply it to the present world.

This inventory shall thus be a tentative spiritual view of the foundational givens of the present world. Without an exact stocktaking of this kind, it is absolutely vain to try to act in the political and economic realm. And that is the central error of social Christianity on the economic or the political terrain.[10] Moved by social problems — unemployment, capitalism's injustices, working-class poverty, etc. — Christians have wanted to look for their solutions. And that is very good because of the charity. But it is an error in that it cannot achieve anything. It is a task like wishing to fill a barrel from one end without checking whether it is closed at the other! Under *certain* spiritual, economic, and social *conditions* this work of charity might have some efficacy. But those conditions have not been fulfilled. [Therefore,] on the one hand, let the charity be truly that which Scripture demands, the charity toward the neighbor (and not toward the Worker or the Proletariat), with its immediate and urgent work. On the other hand, let Christians exercise their discernment concerning their times in order to "hold on to what is good and abstain from every kind of evil" (I Thess. 5:21).

*   *   *

I know, after all, the critique: "More investigations, more intellectual research! What we need is to act! What we are waiting for is a call to action!" There would be much to say about this reaction, which is particularly lively among today's youth. But in the face of this thirst for action, which is perfectly legitimate, I will note only three insights:

The first is that at present this is one of the forms of the world's temptations. "No matter what it is necessary to do, let us act." This is the spring behind every fascism, every dictatorship. Action for its own sake, without any thought to direct it, abandoned as it is to the hands of a supreme director, who in this case is Satan, is a major characteristic of our times. It is odd to see Christians picking up this theme, even though it is precisely said to them, "Do not be conformed to the present age, but be transformed." What is called for is not to do nothing, but rather not to act according to the modes of the present age.

---

10. "Social Christianity" is in France a loose counterpart to the "Social Gospel" movement in the United States. It still exists today in France and publishes *Autre temps* ("Other Times").

The second [insight] is that Scripture teaches us that action depends strictly on thought — and more exactly, that the action of the Christian depends on his theology. Good works are not possible without good theology. The two things are linked — not automatically, but by God himself. Note I Tim. 1:3-10 or Titus 1:5-16 or II Pet. 2; in every case the person with "false doctrine" is at the same time an agent of death. Theological error commands moral sin, one could say. This close dependence, which ought to be studied, is a warning to us: there is no Christian action possible without our knowing exactly what God expects from us, without a work of intellectual and spiritual elaboration on the subject of the action to take.

The third [insight] is that we are in a time which progressively clarifies situations and obliges us to take seriously this constant affirmation of the Scriptures: it matters less to *do* than to *be*. What is important, for example, is not to act purely or justly, but rather to be pure and to be just. Now this is singularly crucial in a world that is going in exactly the other direction; for in our time everyone is concerned to do, to act, and to put one's mark on things and on people, but one is preoccupied very little with being — or rather, one learns to be nothing more than a machine destined to act. It is necessary that Christians today relearn what it means to be. [They must learn] how that requires a certain acting and a certain thinking — but how this thinking is part of their being (and can by no means be disincarnate; that is why we can reverse the previous proposition [and say it is] impossible to have a good theology unless you are saved by Jesus Christ) and how this action is but an expression, temporary and incidental, of their being.

In short, this inventory should have as its goal to provide the elements for thinking sanely about our times, in order to live a Christian life in a concrete way in the midst of our present difficulties and in order to act through our own life. We shall see elsewhere as we move on that indeed there is no act in the present world other than life itself.

TRAJECTORIES

This first article in the series "Chronicle of the Problems of Civilization" is extremely important for understanding the directions that Ellul's life and work took. What he emphasizes "by way of warning" is the need to look beneath the reality of exterior problems in order to find their profound truth. Throughout his life Ellul believed that these fundamental structures had to be understood in order to stop simply plastering up the "accidents" of inequalities and other social problems. When Ellul says that he hoped "later to justify this claim that our time is incommensurable with the rest of history and that the dilemma posed is an authentic one without loophole and without compromise" (p. 15), he was outlining his own tasks for the future of detailing the consequences of what he calls Technique. His books entitled *The Technological Society* (1954/65), *The Technological System* (1977/80), and *The Technological Bluff* (1988/90) and many of his theological works all emphasize that the turn into the technological milieu was — he says with typical overstatement — as radical a change as the original Fall into sin.

"The Principalities and Powers"

Also on p. 15 Ellul writes that the people of 1946 must make a decision on the question of the **structures** of society. Ellul's use of this term *structures* and later of the word *forces* is especially significant because by those terms he designates and describes his initial understanding of the functioning in the modern world of "the principalities and powers," a biblical notion that undergirds all of his sociological, biblical, and ethical work. In this article Ellul explains that his purpose is to make an inventory of these **forces**, beyond their social and economic forms, which condition life in modern times. "These *forces* are identical throughout the world; they are common to all of civilization; they are independent of human will; they have a reality not easily separable from their temporary form"; and they give to the present age "its radically new character" (pp. 19-20, emphasis added).

When Ellul asserts that his inventory of **forces** cannot exhaust the question or give solutions, since each of his points merits a scientific study of one or several volumes, his remark is demonstrated by the unfolding of his own career. He emphasized that before a solution can be sought, a method must be found, and before the method can be sought, the problem must be accurately posed — and then he spent the rest of his life trying to pose the problem of these forces (p. 20). The problem is that our age is characterized by a radical separation of the material and spiritual domains. This societal separation prohibits seeking fundamental spiritual causes for economic or political problems (p. 20).

The fact that Ellul links spiritual causes with economic and political problems in this article from 1946 is especially significant. It demonstrates that from the beginning he based his career on this dialectical understanding: that his separate tracks of theology and *sociologie* had a profoundly deep connection, and that the biblical notion of "the principalities and powers" is that correlating link (and therefore can be for us a key for understanding all that Ellul does).

The connection first came to my attention because of the section on "the powers" in *The Ethics of Freedom*, in which Ellul lists the following possibilities of interpretation for this biblical notion:

> Are they demons in the most elemental and traditional sense? Are they less precise powers (thrones and dominions) which still have an existence, reality, and, as one might say, objectivity of their own? Or do we simply have a disposition of [human beings] which constitutes this or that human factor a power by exalting it as such . . . ? In this case the powers are not objective realities which influence man from without. They exist only as the determination of man which allows them to exist in their subjugating otherness and transcendence. Or finally, at the far end of the scale, are the powers simply a figure of speech common to the Jewish-Hellenistic world, so that they merely represent cultural beliefs and have no true validity?[1]

Ellul situates himself somewhere between the second and third interpretations, for these reasons:

---

1. Jacques Ellul, *The Ethics of Freedom*, trans. and ed. Geoffrey W. Bromiley (Grand Rapids: William B. Eerdmans, 1976), pp. 151-52. Page references to this book in the following discussion are given parenthetically in the text.

On the one side, I am fully convinced with Barth and Cullmann that the New Testament *exousiai* and the power of money personified as Mammon correspond to authentic, if spiritual, realities which are independent of [human] decision and inclination and whose force does not reside in the [person] who constitutes them. Nothing that I have read to the contrary has had any great cogency for me. . . . On the other side, however, the powers do not act simply from outside after the manner of Gnostic destiny or a *deus ex machina*. They are characterized by their relation to the concrete world of [human beings]. According to the biblical references they find expression in human, social realities, in the enterprises of [human beings]. In this sense the occasion of their intervention is human decision and action. (152)

This position is a significant one, for it names the principalities and powers as entities outside of human beings and yet closely linked with human and social realities. Immediately thereafter, in one of his most personal passages on the subject, Ellul describes this connection between the powers and social realities:

Political power has many dimensions, e.g., social, economic, psychological, ethical, psycho-analytical, and legal. But when we have scrutinized them all, we have still not apprehended its reality. *I am not speaking hastily or lightly here but as one who has passed most of his life in confrontation with their question and in their power.* We cannot say with Marx that the power is an ideological superstructure, for it is always there. *The disproportion noted above leads me to the unavoidable conclusion that another power intervenes and indwells and uses political power, thus giving it a range and force that it does not have in itself.*

The same is true of money . . . [and] technology. (153-54, emphasis added)

In my dissertation research,[2] I discovered that this consciousness of the powers and their relationship to social realities undergirds all of Ellul's critical social assessments, though he couched his perceptions in such terms as "necessity" because of his firm conviction that to bring

2. See Marva J. Dawn, "The Concept of 'The Principalities and Powers' in the Works of Jacques Ellul" (Ph.D. diss., University of Notre Dame, 1992).

traditional religious references into the academic milieu of *sociologie* was inappropriate. His insistence that he speaks out of a lifelong confrontation with the question of the powers shows us that the concept provides an important key for interpreting his work.

The dialectic of Ellul's two tracks of work is linked by the powers in that he wants the hope and grace of his theology to be related to the concrete situation of the powers at work in the world. On the other hand, he insists that only on the basis of true freedom through faith is he "able to hold at arm's length these powers which condition and crush me . . . [and to] view them with an objective eye that freezes and externalizes and measures them" (228-33). Among those powers which Ellul specifically listed in *The Ethics of Freedom* and which he himself objectively assessed were the modern state, social utility, money, and the technological society (234, 256).

Ellul's second major theological book, *The Presence of the Kingdom* (1948/51), also laid much groundwork for understanding his perspectives on the concept of "the principalities and powers." Immediately on the second page of the text Ellul discussed the powers by stressing that Christians, by virtue of their relationship with Christ, are confronted by the spiritual forces of the world. Citing Ephesians 6:12 several times in the book, he emphasized equally both the freedom from the fatality of the world that communion with Christ creates and the result of his liberation that we "*can* fight against the spiritual realities of the world."[3]

We cannot in this book trace the progression of the notion of the "powers" throughout Ellul's corpus, but if the reader remembers it as the link between his two tracks of work, then the brutality of Ellul's *sociologie* becomes undergirded with the hope of his Christian faith, and that faith has practical (and more effective) application in response to the troubles of our society. The link is made clear in few of Ellul's works; *The Humiliation of the Word* (1981/86) is a notable and very helpful exception. Though Ellul's own perspective on the *being* of the powers changed between such earlier works as *Money and Power* (1954/85) and one of his later books, *The Subversion of Christianity* (1984/86), his most important contribution was his emphasis on recog-

3. Jacques Ellul, *The Presence of the Kingdom,* trans. Olive Wyon (New York: Seabury Press, 1967), p. 8.

nizing the powers by their **functioning** through such contemporary realities as technology, politics, and economics.

Other Important Themes in "Chronicles" I

Ellul's response to the inevitable criticism that his work is pessimistic (pp. 16-17) is a constant theme in his work. We will read his specific article on that subject in Chapter 4. The themes of being a neighbor and of discernment by genuine Christian realism, introduced on pp. 17-18, will both be expanded in Article 3.

We should also notice in this first major article Ellul's incipient protest against "systems." He emphasizes here (pp. 18-19) that the work of understanding the **structures** of the world in light of the Revelation must be constantly redone, for it can never be enclosed in a theological, political, or economic system, since the world is always changing. Ellul sounded this call for new assessments throughout his career, which is one of the main reasons that he resisted the notion of "disciples" of his own work. We will trace the trajectory of this idea more thoroughly in the comments following Article 3.

A final theme introduced in this article that plays a large part in Ellul's future work is his response to the critique that his comments are just intellectual pursuits when what is really necessary is action (p. 21). His recognition that such a quest for action is one of the forms of the temptations of the world is expanded perhaps most extensively in his later explication of the functioning of the powers in *The Subversion of Christianity* (1984/86). That book laments the many ways in which the true message of Christ has been co-opted by the institution of Christendom and its actions in political and economic realms, by its philosophical and moral systems.

When Ellul reminds us of the scriptural emphasis that Christian action depends on thought, on theology (p. 22), he introduces a main theme of *The Presence of the Kingdom,* which appeared two years after this article (1948/51). In that book, Ellul specifies that the first form of action for the Christian must be a realistic assessment (which means Christian realism) of social and political conditions. In this article, Ellul's next reminder of the constant affirmation of Scripture that it is a matter less of *doing* than of *being* (p. 22) introduces the theme of "incarnating"

27

the will of God through who Christians are, which is also expanded extensively in *Presence*.

We must note, finally, the closing statement of this first major article that Ellul's "inventory should have as its goal to provide the elements for thinking sanely about our times, in order to live a Christian life in a concrete way in the midst of our present difficulties and in order to act through our own life." That is an excellent summary of the connection of the various strands of Ellul's work. His underlying recognition of the workings of the principalities and powers is one of the main elements necessary for "thinking sanely" about the difficulties of our times, so that Christians can respond not only materially but spiritually to the economic, political, and technological problems that Ellul's *sociologie* elaborates. His biblical studies and ethical works describe the Christian life and spur believers to greater faithfulness in response to the freedom of the gospel. Along the way, Ellul's corpus contains many weaknesses and mis- or overstatements, but these basic directions in his work have stimulated, for both believers and nonbelievers, new levels of thinking and living.

CHAPTER 2

"Needed: A New Karl Marx!" (Problems of Civilization II)

SOURCES

Jacques Ellul discovered Marx when he was eighteen. He was a law student and also supporting his parents because his father was unemployed. When both his parents suddenly fell ill, it fell to him besides to care for them and do the household tasks. At that time, reading Karl Marx's *Das Kapital* had a profound effect on him. (He was fluent in German and had been tutoring young students in Latin, Greek, German, and French since he was sixteen to provide the family finances.[1]) As Ellul explains his encounter with Marx,

> I discovered a global interpretation of the world, the explanation for this drama of misery and decadence that we had experienced. The excellence of Marx's thinking, in the domain of economic theory, convinced me. . . . [I]t was the first breakthrough giving me a general interpretation of the world, my first general education.[2]

1. Ellul's father spoke five languages fluently, and his mother was a skilled painter. Both were from wealthy (and foreign) families who had lost their wealth. His father's unemployment was more difficult because, having an aristocratic background and having been a senior executive, he found other job possibilities scarce even before the stock market crash of 1929.
2. Jacques Ellul, *In Season, Out of Season: An Introduction to the Thought of Jacques Ellul,* based on interviews by Madeleine Garrigou-Lagrange, trans. Lani K.

Ellul remained influenced by Marxist thought throughout his life, but he came to recognize its limitations. When asked at age 70, he described his break, not with Marxism, but with its ideology, as follows:

[I broke] with the kind of Marxism that claims to be the aim of and the key to everything. On the other hand, I totally agree with a Marxism that offers a method of interpretation. . . . I also agree with a Marxism that provides some opportunity for political action. All the while, I recognize the dangers of Marxism that were already present in Marx's writing.

. . . Marxism as a sociological study of capitalism does not imply any belief. Belief comes into play, first, when Marxism takes on a messianic, revolutionary dimension . . . and, second, when it is considered a science in every domain. In reality it is pure belief to call Marxism a science. This belief is always dangerous. I can no longer truly believe that Marxism represents the ultimate in science, the ultimate in truth. In these areas I would say that, on the contrary, when Marxism becomes dogmatic it is actually a lie.[3]

Ellul had recognized that Marx did not represent ultimate truth during his involvement, along with his best friend Bernard Charbonneau, in the personalist movement (from 1934-37), but his radical break with Marxism unfolded in the concrete experiences of "the Spanish communists against the anarchists during the war; the activity of underground communists against the underground noncommunists in 1944."[4]

In the following call for a rethinking of the fundamental structures of society, Ellul's critique of the utopian literature of the late 1940s is certainly applicable to our situation at the end of the twentieth century. When he describes the "fever" characterizing the society of his time, we must think of the various fevers afflicting our world at the millennial turn. And who will be the new Karl Marx that we need now?

Niles (San Francisco: Harper & Row, 1982), p. 11. Most of the biographical information in this introduction is taken from this book.

3. Ellul, *In Season*, pp. 60-61.
4. Ellul, *In Season*, p. 61.

Needed: A New Karl Marx!
(Problems of Civilization II)

Jacques Ellul

The literature of these last [few] years, particularly in France since the [1945] liberation, abounds in political, economic, and sociological books, all of which have for a goal French, European, or worldwide reconstruction, [through such means as] the building of new states, of unprecedented systems for the distribution of wealth, and the organization of the peace. However, one should not think that this fact is peculiar to France; Anglo-Saxon authors compete in imagination toward this goal. It is right to say "imagination," for that is the most remarkable and common trait of all of these books: they speculate on a subject known *a priori;* they are strictly utopias. But they have a different look from the classical utopia. Our modern works are serious, overcrowded with statistics, investigations, paragraphs, and notes. They present themselves as scientific works, and not as novels or social satires. Nevertheless, they have no objective value. Their authors demonstrate much imagination and much economic or political knowledge, yet they show equally that they have no knowledge of reality, the reality of human beings or the reality of our civilization. Each has his own idea and constructs a society around that idea, strongly supported with administrative evidence and with figures, which one can always find as needed amid the proliferation of statistics. Indeed, all our authors unanimously take off from their idea of reconstruction, or of rebuilding a new world; and this is evident in two ways. In the first place, in general they each have only a single idea, and we can say without

"Problèmes de Civilisation II: On Demande un Nouveau Karl Marx," *Foi et Vie* 45, 3 (May/June 1947): 360-74.

fear of error that this [lone answer] is quite insufficient amid the complexity of our times. In the second place, this idea always leads to a social form so flawless, so finished, so absolute that one must come to doubt whether it might ever be applicable. It appears as an ideal — but we have learned to mistrust the ideal. In summary, all this accumulation of studies delivered as nourishment to the "cultivated public" appears as a mosaic of ideologies, without any cohesion with reality (for a statistic is not at all a point of cohesion!), [appears] as a pileup of utopias.

Now a difference exists between these projects[1] and [authentic] utopias — to the advantage of the latter. When reading More,[2] Swift,[3] Montesquieu,[4] and any others, one can scarcely mistake the utopian character of their object; yet, when we approach this arid contemporary literature, it is presented with such seriousness, such apparent objectivity, such solidity that we cannot help asking whether we are being faced with applicable projects. And that is the eminent danger of this literature: it switches minds and activities onto sidetracks, whereas the character of the authentic utopias was precisely to discern the main highways leading to future destinations.

Should they then be radically condemned? As far as implementation is concerned, of course! And it is not worth wasting one's time reading all these apprentice dictators. But we are quite obliged to take account of their existence — and the number of these texts gives them an authentic sociological character (one reason more not to believe their intrinsic quality: each of these authors, in writing

---

1. We must note that although Ellul is responding to a considerable number of writings, which he calls "utopian" and which he characterizes well, he never names a specific author. As will be typical in his later works, he paints the general social canvas with broad brush strokes rather than engaging specific writers.

2. Sir Thomas More (1478-1535) served in the British parliament and, during an absence as envoy to Flanders, sketched (in Latin) his description of the imaginary island of "Utopia," a work that was published in 1516.

3. Jonathan Swift (1667-1745), English satirist, born in Ireland, wrote numerous satirical political and ecclesiological pamphlets and is best known for *Gulliver's Travels* (1726).

4. Charles Louis de Secondat, baron of la Brède and of Montesquieu, a French philosophical writer on history (1698-1755).

his system, is obeying not a vocation but sociological trends). This is why all this proliferation offers a meaning. These utopias are a sign that must be understood and interpreted in order to recognize one of the tendencies of our contemporary world. Indeed, a utopia can only be born when it corresponds to a social necessity, and I believe that it is even an excellent thermometer of a society. It is incontestable that the present activity of utopianists shows that we are running a fever of at least 104 degrees. And the fact that these books sell shows that it is not only the utopianists who have the fever.

The abundance of these plans, of these projects teaches us at first the demand of all the people of our era finally to see solutions appear, finally to see a possible path open up. And it is true that what we all suffer from today is not knowing where we are going (for we almost always have *had the impression* of knowing!), and not perceiving any valid reason to hope and to act — this is why we see so many [people] adhering tepidly to communism, the last resort of lost illusions. If we had a better world toward which to march, we would march. But so far, they offer technical solutions to political and economic problems. And the trend still continues, vigorously, "to technical problems, technical solutions." This becomes concrete today, for example, in Econometrics.[5] But it is more and more clearly evident that political and economic problems, even in their most abstract aspect, are never purely technical problems. There always enters a human element that somehow skews the system a bit and that cannot be reduced to an algebraic formulation (although this [human] resistance should not be exaggerated, and it is quite possible today to "accomplish" this!). But it also seems that so-called technical solutions are no longer completely technical because, like it or not, they impose profound consequences on the individual person. At the extreme, one can say that the concentration camp is a technical solution to police, administrative, military, and even economic problems. Nevertheless it contains another element that cannot be eliminated. It is

5. This was a school, connected with Jean Monnet, that applied mathematical analysis to economics. Monnet played important roles in international commerce and in initiating plans that led to the first European Community.

exactly the same for the Beveridge, Full Employment, [and] Social Security plans, etc., etc.[6]

It is undeniable that technical solutions, without being inexact, are inadequate for our questions, very simply because [we think that] they are only technical and are incapable of perceiving that they contain something else, in themselves, which they disregard voluntarily.

On the other hand, in claiming to be technical they are inevitably partial, fragmentary. One cannot conceive of a general technical solution to the economic Problem, for example. There is not [just] one economic problem, but hundreds of them, each with its solution, and one attempts more or less clumsily to make all of these particulars fit together. This fragmentary character is very serious at the very time when precisely there is no longer a deep bond between institutions nor internal cohesion in the society. The abusive application of technique to the social [situation] produces a more and more rapid disintegration of the society. Presently, all of the economic plans — whether they be nationalizations or return to the free market; planning or psychological shock, etc. — have an explosive power on society that accelerates its collapse, and that is precisely because all these plans can envisage only separated questions, which one attempts to harmonize all together by a vague ideological tint.

Finally, technical solutions have one last vice that cannot be eliminated. It is that, presently, all the questions are brought before the grand public, and that all the arrangements of the State have repercussions on private life. The average person, then, does not look at things from a technical point of view, but from her own personal perspective, the repercussions on her situation and her life. Technical solutions leave her quite indifferent, for she does not know how to measure their effects abstractly. This is why these means wear out rapidly: the everyday person expects immediate and miraculous effect from, for example, every new method of resourcing or of reconstruction. If these effects are not produced within

6. The Beveridge plans cited in Chapter 1 were part of the discussions going on in Europe during these postwar years. Pastor Bernard Charles says that Ellul was more aware of the international discussions than many other French people.

forty-eight hours, he stiffens and demands change. It must, moreover, be well recognized that the everyday person is essentially the one who reads the papers or the party member. He will not accept long-term measures unless he is anchored in the idea of the excellence of these measures by something other than their technical value: by some sentimental, mystical, or other reason.

Now we have no more mystique. Even that of the communists seems to be smoldering now in all the countries of the world. In Russia they had to add religion and patriotism during the war, to resuscitate the wobbly communist faith. It seems that after this orgy of mystical exaltation we have just been through in the last fifteen years, the use of this political means[7] no longer has much of a future. People today are more and more resistant to excitement, for they have undergone too much. What is being awaited is rather a reason to live, to act, to advance. A reason that would validate the technical procedures. The modern utopias are a sign of this expectation.

But thus far [the utopias] do not seem to have been able to formulate this reason. They do not answer this expectation. They even all appear extremely laughable in proportion to the demands of people and the complexity of the questions.

While seeking to be founded on concrete data, they are completely disconnected from the real and do not offer any solution. Indeed, they have a totally ambiguous and equivocal character. They reject for the future the construction of a rational world, based on the technical data of today's world; they seek to give persons a reason to live at the same time that they attempt fragmentary solutions to present problems; they count implicitly on the human being without appealing for the person's individual commitment, and are presented as an action plan, which would be realized by some kind of historical alchemy, without anyone's needing to act. These three internal contradictions [separated by semi-colons in the preceding sentence] are found in all the contemporary attempts. They hold a common basic attitude, which can be defined as follows:

7. The phrase "this political means" refers to the "mystique" of ideologies, such as fascism, the Spanish Civil War, World War II, communism, etc.

One can act only for rational motives, and the society of the future must be conceived rationally. All the progress of history is, ultimately, progress toward greater rationalization of administration, of the state, of the economy (this notion being perfectly accepted even in the political theories one calls irrational, like nazism). It is necessary therefore to establish plans that are more and more rational and precise, and to act according to these plans. That alone seems motive enough to act. But this rationalistic conception expresses itself principally in the idea that all problems are [problems] of detail and that adding up solutions of detail will give the general solution. (And here the modern utopias obey the mentality of technique, and that is why they utilize technical data so abundantly.) And further, if one is located exactly in the flow of history, our system will fulfill itself (a vague Marxist residue that all of the utopias entail more or less — even those on the right). A person is at bottom no more than one accessory factor, and one cannot count so much on the action of the individual as on the action of the mass, which alone is taken into consideration by history.

On the foundation of this attitude, our utopianists bring their solutions. But their solutions to what? That is one of the most suggestive surprises there might be, which one experiences in reading these essays. Nobody is concerned to know the problem. One begins with the very general and vague idea: "it's not working." What? Everything: the economic, the political, the social. More precisely? Unimportant. Vain analyses, mind games. What is needed is a remedy, and that right away. Not a single one of these texts has tried really to diagnose in a precise and synthetic way the questions of the modern world. All are satisfied with two antithetical and equally false elements: the vague feeling of malaise mentioned above and the technical description of problems of detail. Now these problems are all, without exception, wrongly posed because [they are] isolated from the rest, because [they are] isolated from their human foundation, because [they are] conceived in accordance with general ideas or conceptions more than a century old, because [they are] conceived as causes when they are only effects.

Consequently our utopianists commit two sizable medical errors: choice of remedies without having a diagnosis of the malady; treating the external symptoms and not the reality they express. And this is why I have designated their work as pure imagination.

To begin at the beginning, we must try to pose clearly the foundational problems.

We find ourselves thus in the presence of a large number of solutions, but these do not respond to any problem posed — or more precisely, the problem is posed well enough in the reality, in the practical life, but it is not formulated, it is not intellectually, analytically conceived. Now it is impossible to answer a question when the question is not thus posed. We have to come back to these infinitely simple things, in a time when people no longer know how to see things simply. I will not say that technical pursuits, in the social or political domains, are useless, but [I will say] that they do not respond to a problem because they are merely instruments for resolving the problem. What demonstrates this quite curiously is that now we reach the following conclusion: one tackles a minuscule social problem, one finds for it the best possible technical solution, and then one notices that this technical solution presupposes calling into question all of society, the economic and political structure, etc.; thus the plan for social security (which despite appearances is the response only to a very small question!) presupposes transforming the tax structure, the structure of corporations, working conditions, the structure of society (diminution of the number of farmers, disappearance of the middle class), the conception of the role of the state, etc.; every problem posed technically brings in its train the upheaval of the whole of society. But one can understand that this "chain reaction" of disintegration, beginning at the smallest end, is not a good method to respond to contemporary social needs.

Consequently, if we reject the two procedures proposed — namely, the technical step, which beginning with a small question, arrives indirectly, by way of consequences and repercussions, at a modification of the entire society, and the utopian step, which concocts solutions, envisions them on a grand scale, and descends from there to the technical precision — what else remains?

*   *   *

We find a precedent for our situation in the period that goes from 1815 to 1848.[8] I understand this precedent from the viewpoint of the attitude of the people of that time in the face of the political, economic, and social situation. In that moment, too, we encounter people who attempt technical solutions and people who attempt to reconstruct society beginning with a utopia. Now precisely, the utopia of the early nineteenth century presents nearly the same characteristics as our own. Think among others of Saint-Simon[9] or of Fourier[10]; they had a utopia buttressed by economic knowledge and apparently applicable. So there we are in the presence of an attempt to put problems back into place, the total and global reconstruction of society, but in reality work that is done beginning with nothing and responding effectively to nothing. At the most, we can say that that [work] created a climate, but even this we can say today [only] because those utopianists were followed by Proudhon[11] and by Karl Marx. If it had not been for those two men, the utopian socialists of the early nineteenth century would today be known only to a few graduate scholars needing a dissertation topic. Our contemporary utopianists are destined for total oblivion, because they do not have the breadth of the others and because there seems to be no new Karl Marx on the horizon. Today it seems necessary to find a new Karl Marx.

Marx was the only man of his time who grasped the totality of the social, political, and economic problems in their reality and posed correctly the questions [facing] the civilization of the nineteenth century. This is not to say that the answers given by him were correct, that the double historical extrapolation[12] he

8. 1815 was the year of the Treaty of Vienna, the restoration of the monarchy as a reaction to the French Revolution; 1848 refers to revolutions in several Western European countries (France, Germany, Austria, Hungary, Italy).

9. Claude Henri of Rouvroy, the count of Saint-Simon (1760-1825), a French social philosopher.

10. Ellul may mean François Marie Charles Fourier (1772-1837), French socialist and reformer.

11. Pierre Joseph Proudhon (1809-1865), French socialist and writer.

12. [Ellul's footnote:] Double extrapolation: one toward the past, which consists in saying that all societies are explained by the same means as that of the nineteenth century, and one toward the future, which consists in saying that the future society will have to be constructed on the bases offered by that of the nineteenth century.

made was right, that the philosophy he applied was eternal, or that his sudden awareness and his construction, which were valid in the middle of the nineteenth century, are still that in the middle of the twentieth century. It suffices, for the greatness of Marx, that he was truly the man who mastered his epoch and was able to make the synthesis of the enormous amount of material that had been provided him.

Now what is it that made the enormous success and influence of Karl Marx? It is neither the easiness of [reading] his works and their popular or propagandistic character, nor his revolutionary activity, nor the "chiefs of staff" who surrounded him, nor the devotion of working-class leadership:[13] it is essentially the fact that the diagnosis he posited was true. The fact that he remained attached to the real, and that he was able to see it in its profound reality — one might say, objectively. Behind the phenomena that faced him, he was able to discern what was [its] profound tendency. Among the facts, he knew how to choose what was essential and leave what was accidental. Then he worked with the totality of political and economic phenomena; he knew how to consider them in their internal relations; he did not let himself be misled by superficial historical causality, and, taking hold of these bundles of events and their relations, he knew how to pose the veritable questions of the nineteenth century in all their breadth and their difficulty.

However, his work is no longer valid. General conditions have changed as much in one century as [they had] in the three centuries that preceded Marx. Those who today still lean on Marx are laggards, reactionaries who have not understood precisely what is the real grandeur of Marx. But a work like his is essentially ephemeral. For it loses its value when the conditions that brought it to birth change. (And it is that which he wished to avoid in creating a philosophical system that is at the very least dubious.) Should one say, then, that it was wasted effort to invest all that genius for nothing but a temporary restatement? Certainly not, for it is this restatement, this deep stock-taking about an epoch, which influenced the course of history more than anything else. It is of little

13. Ellul is probably being sarcastic, since none of these things was strong.

enough importance to insist today on applying the Marxist system, which is no longer adequate, but it is of great importance that Marx polarized history during approximately a century. For if we wish it or not, we are obliged to refer to this polarization in order to understand the history of these last hundred years.

However, today everything has changed. Political givens, psychological and spiritual givens, social givens, intellectual and scientific givens, economic givens. Nothing more among the facts serves any longer as a basis for the Marxist system. And it always has an extraordinary effect to see a vocabulary used that took account of reality a century ago and that, having remained the same, is also as far as possible from the present situation.

What seems absolutely necessary today is to do again precisely the same work that Karl Marx did a hundred years ago. Only thus can we have a hope of seeing more clearly in our situation. Only thereby will the utopias appear as the preparatory groundwork and will the technical solutions find their place.

However, it is necessary not to have any illusions. The work is more complicated [now] than a century ago, for everything has become more complex, and who will have the genius of Marx?

While waiting, we can try to prepare the task, to sketch the problem.

What are the requirements, such as we can see them, in what Marx did?

First of all, it is necessary to know the ensemble of the phenomena, to have an encyclopedic view of our time. This assumes an obvious superficiality. However, by no means can it be an incoherent knowledge or a mixture without order. The encyclopedism in question is there only to provide the elements of a precise and thorough analytical knowledge. It corresponds neither to the *World Book Encyclopedia*[14] nor to a contemporary secondary education. One must know an immense quantity of facts in order to find what is truly significant and what must be both retained and studied. This encyclopedism is absolutely necessary, since no specialization will permit one to take into account the questions of our civilization. But then

14. Ellul names the *Encyclopédie Larousse*, which is smaller and less complete than the *Encyclopedia Britannica*.

one must know how to get rid of it when the facts have been chosen and one moves on to the second task: their analysis.

This is essentially the analytic method that is presently necessary, for this alone, as Marx has shown, permits a real grasp of the world. [It is] only analysis that should lead to the discovery of basic givens common to the entire civilization. It is indeed in the analysis of current concrete situations that we can find the reality of the problems of our time. These [givens] are not all formulated, they are not evident; only the technical questions are evident, where a discovery automatically engenders an apparent question. The problems of civilization are not evident; they must be deciphered in the warp and woof of historic events of many kinds. It is the most intensive and the deepest analysis of these historic events, selected and kept to specifics, that gives the content of these problems. This is, for example, what Marx did with his investigation of the situation of [factory] workers in England in 1948.

People will ask, then, is a pure intellectual work what is needed? In a certain measure, yes. And it seems to me quite vain to want to dispense with intelligence in order to direct the action and to want to act right away and at any price, without knowing what one is going to do, without previously having sat down to count the cost. Now this is very characteristic of the utopia and of technical solutions: one applies no serious intellectual method, and one seeks immediately to govern the action. It is true that those who possess an intellectual method use it for everything other than the profound knowledge of our times and prefer to smash the atom or to interpret Lucian of Samosata.[15]

And on the other hand, what matters is not exclusively a disinterested intellectual research. It is necessarily comprised between two boundaries. On one side a spiritual attitude *a priori;* on the other, the object: namely, action. No one can avoid the *a priori,* and it is by virtue of this that, for example, the choice of the phenomena in the encyclopedic knowledge will be made. Here again Marx is a good guide, [for] he, too, let himself be led by his spiritual judgment

---

15. Ellul refers sarcastically to this second-century A.D. Greek satirist to show the esoterism of certain intellectual endeavors, which avoid dealing with fundamental questions of meaning.

of things. To say that this is not a scientific attitude is an error. This is not a liberal attitude, but that is not the same thing. What is an anti-scientific attitude is to declare, to the contrary, that one has no *a priori*. I hold that a spiritual position is necessary for an intellectual comprehension of the world. And on the other hand, it is necessary that this comprehension have as its goal, more or less distant, a certain way of living — that is, action, without letting that [goal] diminish the intellectual intransigence.

We need not research further the detail of this method. It seems to me that today this alone can give a result — that [result] being, it is necessary to emphasize, only the clear and correct condition of the problems of our civilization.

*　　*　　*

Thus far I have repeatedly used the terms *structures* or *fundamental givens*. The meaning should be clarified, since the search for these structures will be the object of these articles. Underneath the phenomena that we are able to see in the social, political, economic realms, there are some permanent forces of which the tracks are found in each of the phenomena considered, and which ensure its unity to our times beneath its chaotic and disorderly appearance. Exactly as in a tapestry, there is an unseen warp that ensures the unity of the fabric and that is the foundational element upon which is developed the outward designs and ornaments. It is not a matter, then, of declaring that a certain order of phenomena is fundamental in relation to the others, whereby one would set aside completely what are called *structures* in our present political vocabulary. This word has indeed become fashionable, signifying solely [this] in political thought: economic phenomena. Everyone has come to hold, according to a diluted communism, that in social life the economic facts form the structure of the society. Consequently, to modify the economic system is to change the social life completely. Now what I intend to show here precisely is that the economic system is itself also a superstructure, that the economic facts are themselves external phenomena which do not have reality by themselves. And on the other hand, it will seem evident to us that one can perfectly modify economic life and its regime from top to bottom without changing in the slightest the fundamental structures of society. We are aware, for example, that these structures are exactly the same in a capitalist regime and in a communist regime: the latter can make a certain change of the economic phenomena at a given point, but that is in no way a transformation of the society, a revolution in the civilization. Within the civilization the economy appears as one of the elements of the organism, neither more important than the others, despite our obsessions, nor more decisive as far as the revolution is concerned. Thus we should consider the economic facts, like intellectual and artistic facts, for instance, to discern what are the fundamental structures, but it is not these phenomena nor these economic regimes which are in themselves the structures.

What then are for us the structures? It is necessary to guard against another error, toward which the philosophers are inclined, which is to name permanent, eternal elements of the world as structures. Pushing that to the extreme: "matter" or "human nature" or "the problem of the Society," etc. To the contrary, I will regard as a structure in the question of the civilization that which is specific to modern times, and not at all what is common to every civilization, to every society. Consequently, this research is located between the permanent in the course of all history and the provisional, strictly episodic, and momentary. We will consider, then, in our civilization (that which began to appear in the European West toward the sixteenth century and progressively spread around the whole world) what is singular to it, distinctive compared to the others. We shall not look for more or less indiscreet historical analogies, but we shall watch what gives our modern world its authentic and undeniable character. And on the other hand, we shall try to seek what gives a certain unity to the totality of this civilization, wherever that is manifested, and under whatever regime that might be. This, then, will be a second characteristic of what I call a "fundamental structure": the element common to an entire series of phenomena in our civilization, whatever might be the superficial differences between these phenomena. But on the other hand, it seems clear that if this element is modified, it is the entire civilization which is in fact called into question. This is really what Marx had seen, concerning private property, and that could have been exact, but it is no longer the

43

case, for our civilization is no longer centered on this private property. We have then a third characteristic: "a structure" is that which by its modification brings a radical change, a revolution (in the pre-Marxist sense of the word) in the whole civilization.

Now we understand the necessity of studying these structures if one desires, not even to prepare a new civilization, but only to discern the paths of an authentic revolution. It is because of the failure to recognize this problem of the structures that the techniques and the utopias are equally ineffective. Only one must not imagine, after what I have just said, that these structures are essentially abstract, that they are ideas or principles. On the contrary, actually a structure is necessarily very close to persons. It concerns them directly. If we attempt to distill its quintessence, to arrive at one or several principles, we would be doing the work of the philosopher, which does not concern us, but especially [if we sought principles] we would detach ourselves very rapidly from the reality of the civilization, and we would be diverting our purpose. We will as a matter of fact recognize a structure by a last characteristic, which is that it concerns the individual life of persons. It is only in this measure that it is a structure *of civilization*. If it concerns only the ideas or the indifferent and purely objective facts, we could not give it this name. What will allow us to recognize a structure, then, will not be its material importance, its influence on the economic or political order, but rather its repercussions on the concrete life of the average person. A structure will be what shapes average people, what has a decisive force in the organization of their life, in the order of their thoughts, in their behavior, in their habits. And this reference to the person (even when we discover that such power tends precisely to destroy this person) takes on a singular value in order to determine these structures when we ponder that precisely all these systems make an abstraction of this person. Now it is only in referring to the person that one can truly measure a civilization. It is not the knowledge of heroes or of demigods that gives us the secret of a civilization, but far more [the knowledge] of the everyday person that "Saturday Evening"[16] or the "comics" reveal to us.

16. *Samedi Soir* was the name of a weekend gossip newspaper.

It is in pondering these average people, where they live and whatever might be their race, formed by a universal civilization, that we can distinguish the great forces which hold [in their grasp] this entire civilization.

* * *

Beginning in the next article I shall commence the study of these structures, of which I will give here the list, while taking into consideration that we shall study these givens, not in themselves, but insofar as [they are] structures of civilization. These essential structures seem to me to be: Technique, Production, the State, the City, War, and Sterilization.

TRAJECTORIES

Ellul concludes this second article of the series "Problems of Civilization" with the inventory he promised in the first article. Concerning almost all the structures on the list he wrote one or more full-length studies and often numerous articles besides. The main exceptions are the topics of production and sterilization. Ellul's analyses of the former often occur in the midst of his commentaries on the technological milieu — a good example would be the section on "The Bluff of Productivity" in *The Technological Bluff* (1988/90) — and in his critiques of myths, such as in *The New Demons* (1973/75). Though Ellul himself wrote no major articles on sterilization that I could find, the topic was "in the air" because of Hitler's policies and because of previous European thinkers who had advocated "eugenics" in the pre–World War II period. Certainly now at the end of the century, issues of birth control, abortion, and population management have become incendiary.

Ellul undoubtedly published most on the subject of technique, including hundreds of articles and the sequence of *The Technological Society* (1954/64), *The Technological System* (1977/80), and *The Technological Bluff* (1988/90). Throughout these works he criticizes not technology *per se*, but **Technique.** Ellul does not use this word to signify machines, technology, or particular procedures. Rather, "in our technological society, *technique* is the *totality of methods rationally arrived at and having absolute efficiency* (for a given stage of development) in *every* field of human activity."[1] His critique of technique's autonomy, its self-augmentation, totalization, monism, and universalism, and of technique's connections with economic systems and politics, to the destruction of humanity, is a much-needed assessment in our times.

Ellul's works on "the State" include primarily his books *Propaganda* (1962/65) and *The Political Illusion* (1965/67), although comments on the subject abound in many of his theological works as well. He gave a complete overview of the biblical picture of "the City" and its implications for today's urbanized society in *The Meaning of the City* (published in English first, 1970). On the subject of war Ellul's primary works

---

1. Jacques Ellul, *The Technological Society*, trans. John Wilkinson (New York: Random House, 1964), p. xxv.

include *Autopsy of Revolution* (1969/71) and *Violence* (published in English first, 1969).

Certainly in the breadth of his analysis and in the perspicacity of his vision Ellul served as the new Karl Marx for which he called. Though all of the works noted above no doubt include errors of detail, there is equally no doubt that in their time they presented new, alternative, sometimes caustic perspectives on customarily accepted aspects of society. Many contemporary social and political critics cite Ellul as a model or mentor or initiator of their thought.

Especially in this sound-bite age, we need to imitate Ellul's critique of utopian proposals that show no understanding of reality because they are not complex enough or because they simply posit an ideal, which, if achieved, could solve all of civilization's problems (pp. 31-32). Like half a century ago, today we recognize that the plethora of proposed solutions indicates the immense need for them and that the purely technical solutions offered are necessarily too fragmentary (pp. 33-34). We can verify that the abusive application of technique to social situations has produced increasingly rapid disintegration of society (p. 34). Still we suffer, as Ellul exclaimed, from two medical errors: that we choose remedies without accurately diagnosing the malady and that we treat the exterior symptoms and not the true disease they express (pp. 36-37).

In our present-day need for a new Karl Marx who will pose the questions in view of the entirety of the social situation (pp. 37-38), we must recognize that the work today is even harder than when Ellul first wrote this piece, since the situation is now even more complex. And with the plethora of facts in this information age, how can anyone know the whole ensemble of phenomena and have the encyclopedic view of our times for which Ellul called? Certainly our age of even more minute specializations prohibits taking account of all the facts and questions (p. 40). However, we can follow Ellul's directive in finding the right methods to grasp truly the situation of our world. We can join him in discovering the **particular underlying principles** (p. 41) (the *forces* of the first article in this series) that characterize our present time.

This second article is especially helpful for its clarification (pp. 42-45) of Ellul's use of the term *structures* and the phrase "fundamental givens," which again provide a foundational description of some of the elements of his understanding of the biblical notion of "the principalities and powers." He emphasizes that the tracks of these permanent **forces** are found in the phenomena in the social, political, and economic domains; the forces themselves are (to use Ellul's image) the "unseen warp" of a tapestry upon which is developed the patterns and the exterior ornaments (p. 42). These **structures** are not eternal, like philosophical ideals, but they authentically characterize modern society and also concern the individual life of persons. They are a decisive **force** in the organization of people's lives, the order of their thoughts, their behavior, and their habits. At the same time, however, such **power** tends precisely to annihilate people.

Critics such as Neal Postman have recognized the structural totalitarianism of such aspects of contemporary life as television.[2] But it is important for Christians to remember Ellul's emphasis (hinted at in this and the previous article, but not clearly enunciated until *The Humiliation of the Word*) that these structural forces are analogous to the biblical principalities and powers and therefore must be combatted not only with material techniques but also with spiritual understanding. In fact, our very efforts to deal with such contemporary problems as drug abuse and the widening of the economic gap between the rich and the poor fail because we do not recognize the problems' spiritual roots. Ellul's critique of Technique in this article and throughout his life is especially needed today.

Finally, a very important follow-up to this second article was Ellul's book *Jesus and Marx: From Gospel to Ideology* (1979/88), in which he demonstrates the dangers that arise when the texts of Christianity are given socialist readings. Throughout his life Ellul insisted that Marx and Christ could not be reconciled, even though he had kept his feet in both camps. Indeed, he had introduced courses in Marxist thought at the University of Bordeaux long before they became the popular thing to do. *Jesus and Marx* still retains the positive evaluation of Marxist methods found in this article, but in that book Ellul strongly critiques socialist theologies that are not really theologies because of their conformity to our culture's ideologies.

2. See Postman's book *Amusing Ourselves to Death: Public Discourse in the Age of Show Business* (New York: Viking Penguin, 1985), and also *Technopoly: The Surrender of Culture to Technology* (New York: Alfred A. Knopf, 1992).

CHAPTER 3

"Political Realism"
(Problems of Civilization III)

SOURCES

The list that ended the second article in Ellul's series "Problems of Civilization" outlines much of Ellul's work in hundreds of articles and scores of books over the next forty-seven years. However, he added only one article concerning the items in the inventory to his *Foi et Vie* series — this third article (1947) dealing specifically with the **structure** of politics. In his autobiographical book *Perspectives on Our Age,* Ellul said that he had learned from Marx the importance of grasping all of reality,[1] so we can understand why this article, in which Ellul shows that political realism is not a genuine realism, should follow the previous one on Marx.

Though the article is quite lengthy and sometimes repetitive, it is nonetheless extremely important because Ellul thoroughly distinguishes between political realism, which is actually an illusion and a means of conformity, and authentic Christian realism, which is revolutionary and enables the believer to recognize and combat the functioning of the principalities and powers in the realities of the world. His discussion of primary elements in Christian realism is an excellent summary of biblical

---

1. Jacques Ellul, *Perspectives on Our Age: Jacques Ellul Speaks on His Life and Work,* trans. Joachim Neugroschel, ed. William H. Vanderburg (New York: Seabury Press, 1981), p. 14.

truths to be incarnated in the life of faith. The article thereby summarizes the major motivations for most of Ellul's work in various tracks: he wrote biblical studies to nurture readers' growth in Christian realism, social criticism to help them see the world more realistically, and ethical works to challenge the Church to take up more effectively the tasks of Christian realism.

Political Realism
(Problems of Civilization III)

Jacques Ellul

Today there is no longer the possibility of rejecting political realism. Everyone in our time is a realist, and the highest compliment one can pay politicians is to observe that they are realists. After having been sufficiently disgusted by hypocritical idealism in the genre of Thiers[1] and by mystical idealism [in President Woodrow] Wilson's genre, everyone has now caught hold of a "healthy realism," according to the acknowledged formula. Mr. Molotov[2] is a realist, Mr. Marshall[3] too. But if "realism" designated only a certain type of statesman, or if it were only a more or less vague formula to describe a political style, it would not merit any serious attention. But that is not the case. Realism is a perfectly coherent political notion, which has become integrated into the whole of our civilization, is an integral part of it, [and] tends to give it decisive shape. Realism is a certain conception of the world, and it concerns us all directly.

Without any doubt, it would be ungracious not to grant that this realism is valid and attractive. People have long enough been separated, torn apart, excommunicated, executed for merely ideological

1. Adolphe Thiers was chief executive of the French provisional government, which negotiated a peace treaty with Bismarck in 1871 and against which the Parisian workers revolted in the "commune" of spring, 1871.

2. Vyacheslav Molotov became a minister under Stalin in 1930.

3. George Marshall served as U.S. Army Chief of Staff during World War II and then as U.S. Secretary of State. He designed the Marshall Plan for European reconstruction.

'Problèmes de Civilisation III: Le Realisme Politique," *Foi et Vie* 45, 7 (November/December 1947): 698-734.

reasons, when they were already sufficiently divided for material reasons. Let us then stop adding to our factual divisions [other] divisions that we can invent; let us stop indulging in our imaginative delirium; let us stop considering other people as bearers of lethal spiritual or moral germs, in order to see them as they are: people materially like us. Probably we shall succeed better at understanding one another if we thus free ourselves from these artificial conflicts in order to limit our conflicts to what can truly not be avoided; let us forget our quarrels in order to take stock of our demands.

From another viewpoint, political realism seeks to establish a little coherence in the political problems of our times. It puts its finger on an evident implausibility of previous political systems — how [they thought they would] resolve political and economic problems by means of good feelings or by the application of abstract principles! Every time someone has wanted to apply principles in politics, we have realized that the consequences would be absolutely impossible or quite catastrophic; whether it was the principle of sovereignty, or of natural borders, or of non-intervention, or of the freedom of peoples for self-determination, etc., one could cite them all — these principles have provoked political disasters. It is evident that, since the circumstances of times and of places differ, it is impossible to apply identical principles to everything everywhere. On the contrary, it is advisable to consider each problem as a whole while at the same time attributing importance to each element of the problem. If one begins in this way, one perceives very quickly that each problem is first of all technical and that it is advisable to envisage it under this aspect: for a technical problem, a technical solution. It is no longer a question of settling the issues in the abstract, but of seeing them first in the most concrete way possible and of resolving them according to the necessities of the moment. It is impossible to pursue a serious policy without having studied beforehand all the material aspects of the problem, and it is the combination itself of these givens that will finally furnish the solution. Therefore, in realism there is a praiseworthy effort to "see things as they are," and it is quite evident that the reproaches addressed to the political idealism of the nineteenth century, for example, are too true for us not to be entirely ready to agree with this position, which is also wise, also reasonable and rational. We

52

must not build castles in the air, but must construct them on the solid ground of the facts.

These affirmations are so evident and so widely prevalent in [public] discourse and the press, that today we can take this posture to be common to all the political parties, to all the nations, to all the social classes.

However, realism is quite far from having kept its promises. The solid ground of political and economic facts is beyond doubt itself entirely as unreliable and shifting as that of the ideologies. The conflicts in these realms are just as productive of war as the others, and no more reconcilable. And it is hard to see what has been gained by asserting to the hero of [the battle of] Warnez that he was killed for petroleum or coal, whereas before we would have told him that he was killed for honor or glory. Realistic solutions finally reveal themselves to be just as fragile as the others, and also not "solutions" at all.

But in making these observations, which are accessible to anyone, we are saying basically that realism is no more politically efficacious than idealism, and, saying this, we remain on the terrain of realism's predilections, we judge realistically, and we support the *communis opinio.* We ought to go further.

*   *   *

The components of political realism demonstrate perfectly that it is part of an ensemble of phenomena and that it is by no means an arbitrary stance. We find that it has ideological roots and material roots. But it is necessary to understand more. I do not mean to say that it is the product of an ideological theory, but only [that it is the product] of a current attitude, common to a strong majority of the people of our time.

And at first it is a nearly inevitable result of the observation that there is no such thing as truth. The skepticism of the average person is the precondition of political realism. One no longer recognizes any moral truth; one no longer knows what is good or evil. One no longer recognizes any philosophical or scientific truth. Everything is questioned, as if Descartes were the master of the modern mind, yet one goes no further — one stops after this [general] questioning, and one certainly is not ready to sacrifice for any reason; it is therefore acceptable not to go beyond the stage of political interest,[4] and one will not accept "marching for Danzig"![5] This absence of truth, the conviction at the bottom of all contemporary human relations, this radical relativism, about which we can do nothing, entails a second condition of political realism — namely, submission to the facts. The fact is established, is seen (or is thought to be seen); it cannot be debated. No opinion can stand up in the face of the fact. There is no guide or truth; the fact is justified by itself, and it is sufficient in itself. Fact replaces truth. Everything can be doubted, but not the fact. Consequently, it is the fact that will be the grand law for the average person; it is submission to the fact that will be the current posture. In politics, that is what we call realism. It can no longer be a question of ideological politics because the people no longer have faith in any ideology. It can only be a question of politics as submission to the facts; therein resides the extraordinary vigor of the Marxist method. All problems are attacked only by taking account of the facts, which are interpreted according to the best method possible — that is why there is not any communist truth; there is only a technique for interpreting the facts. Thus the opinion of the average person is in agreement with the highest form of contemporary politics, and one comprehends that this cannot be other than realist. It is impossible to govern in disagreement with public opinion, which only accepts being influenced in the direction of basic tendencies, and that is the failure of all systems. All that is possible is to race after history, [which is nothing but] a succession of little facts that have no rhyme nor reason, seen through the eyes of the everyday person without any larger perspective, [the sort of] history of which our daily press is a rigorous and pathetic reflection.

Where can we stop, then? Why turn to the right or the left? There is no longer any valid reason for us. There is only our situa-

4. That is, it is acceptable to do politics with no reference whatever to scientific, moral, or philosophical truth.
5. The march for Danzig took place after Chamberlain capitulated at Munich in 1938. Pastor Charles says it means "marching for honor," such as trying to "save Sarajevo" would mean in 1996.

tion. The Marxist formula, "there is no human nature; there is only the human condition," expresses a general conviction of contemporary people. And this conviction is also a condition of realism. It is vain to seek a natural order, to want to develop human nature, to place it in a context that is engendered by its nature. All of that seems left behind. And this feeling seems to me [to be] engendered by an extreme unconscious despair. For generations, human beings have been placed in the midst of conditions of life so inhumane that they have lost consciousness of having a nature. It is a matter, not only of conditions that appear bad to us (for example, the slums, bad working conditions for laborers, etc.), but also of [conditions] that are not at all discussed and that nevertheless are inhumane (overcrowding, excessive rapidity of travel, canned foods, substitutes of all kinds, work that is too extensive in all the social classes, social security, entertainment, etc.). To be human today is no longer to know neither one's profound needs nor one's personal desires; we no longer know anything but our situation, our condition, and we adopt the needs and the desires of our condition. We no longer expect politics that is a defense of humankind, but only a defense of our situation, whatever it is — juridical, political, economic, social — and thereby we want nothing but politics that responds to the material condition, that takes into consideration only this fact.

It would be easy to pursue further this analysis of the mentality of the average contemporary person; these summary indications suffice to show how realistic politics is deeply rooted in the psychology, the prejudices, the sentiments of those governed and [thus] cannot provoke any scandal. But it is also swept along by the phenomena that can be called objective, such as nationalism and the primacy of the economy. Every nationalistic politics must be realist, for every nationalistic politics is dominated by the spirit of power, and that could not put up with any queenly virtue. When nationalism has become the final rationale in a nation, then politics is no longer anything but an instrument of grandeur for the nation. It no longer has a rule to follow; it no longer has anything but services to render. Now, everyone presently obeys [such] a real nationalism, even the internationalists. And there can no longer be an idealistic politics; that would lead only to monstrous impasses. A very clear example is furnished by the Wilsonian rule of the freedom of peoples for self-determination: an excellent idea, but inapplicable in a world given over to nationalism. It is not the peoples but the nations who decided; the democratic principle played the game of diverse autocracies. Thus Mr. Bidault could recently pronounce at Moscow the funeral oration for this principle, with everyone agreeing.[6] Nationalism brings with itself the rejection of all political principles, and one key to political realism is the choice of only those means that will give free course to [nationalism's] desire for power.

The other key is the primacy of the economic over the political. All agree easily today on the fact that the political cannot be normative, that it is entirely based on the economic life, that it is conditioned by it, and that one need not bother having theories, that it suffices to attend directly to the management of the economy. All political wisdom is summarized in this reflection of the economic. It is not necessary to insist on showing how this posture is consistent with realism. The economy appears as the substance itself on which political action is exerted, but a substance that dominates the exertion by far. There cannot exist any political humaneness; we are in the realm of things, and it is now for the sake of things that politics is done.

All of this says that realism is not a vague tint of politics or an accident, but that it belongs powerfully and entirely to our times. If we are to question this posture, we must know what we are attacking, and [we must realize] that it is not at all a quarrel about terms or ideas, but about the very force, the very blood of the world in which we live.

*   *   *

Today this power is no longer even discussed. It forms a whole, it impregnates the commonplaces and the highest politics, it is prop-

---

6. Georges Bidault, president of the National Council of the Resistance, became the chief of French diplomats under de Gaulle and then the head of the ministry of foreign affairs. In March of 1947, at the conference of the four world powers in Moscow, Stalin's obstinacy concerning the Saar in Georgia led to changes in French policy.

agated by all the periodicals of all the parties, it is the philosophy of our times. It carries within itself its own criteria, and this is not its least singularity. All actions today are measured by realism, and the measure that the latter imposes on them is success. It cannot be otherwise because of the predominance of the "fact." "Fact" having become a veritable god, it is by the factual consequences that we calculate the value of an action. What matters now is no longer the right or the true or the beautiful, but the fact: and accordingly, everything that has no factual consequences is without importance; everything that does not change the factual situation is without value. We ought to succeed — and to succeed in the sole realm of the facts; it is that which becomes the criterion of all actions, and that, obviously, is why all the philosophies and all the arts are obsolete. We question ourselves indefinitely and with anguish concerning the abandonment of all culture by the people, concerning the separation between the arts and the people, to the impoverishment of both. But there is only one explanation [for that impoverishment], which any person in the crowd will give you [by asking]: "What does it serve?" The realism common to all that dominates politics demands that "it" serve, and rigorously, that it reach some material success; thus all the scientific inventions and all the psychological, sociological, and metaphysical discoveries have been made to serve, for the greater well-being of humankind, for total war, and for the totalitarian State.

The criterion of success, of utility, of interest. One can scarcely find another motive for action today — what succeeds is justified; what fails is criminal. And just as the realist bourgeois thought at the dawn of our modern times that poverty is the product of vice (Guizot[7]), even so only the thread of [the Allies'] victory kept the criminals of Nüremberg from being celebrated as the greatest men of our times. No doubt this conception has always been more or less present in history, but previously it was implicitly connected with the mystery of the judgment of God [as that was] misunderstood. God caused the failure of the

---

7. François Guizot (1787-1874), Protestant and principal minister of Louis Philippe (of the July Monarchy in 1840), wrote what might be called the Whig history of the French.

projects of the one who did wrong, and consequently success or failure would come from a decision of God, would be the outward proof of their righteousness or wickedness. Today it is quite evident that this interpretation has been completely erased, despite the old superstitious vestiges that make [people] believe that civilization must triumph over barbarity and progress over obscurantism. The final ground of our realism is truly the most concrete, the most immediate utility, and actions are justified no longer by an objective judgment, but by interest. American moralistic propaganda is based entirely on the axiom: "crime does not pay." The operation is not profitable; therefore, be moral. Unfortunately, if one shows that crime does pay, then one ought immediately to become criminal.

"If you pay for your ride, you will help the service" one reads in the busses where there is no ticket-taker but only a coin box. Unfortunately, it is never anything but a question of interest, and all [we need] is to know whether the collective interest outweighs the personal interest. On this foundation, the criterion of realism is success, but a success that is visible, concrete, immediate, measurable, about which one cannot quibble: a success in the facts. The true realistic politics is that of the boxer who knocks out his adversary: no discussion. And consequently it is necessary to succeed by all means, using all resources to arrive at this goal. But, after all, what goal? That is of little importance. We no longer choose our goals, measure our ends, calculate the objective; the bigger and nearer the goal is, the more chance there is of being attained, therefore the more it is desirable. Our goal is no longer "ours"; it is what the objective facts objectively propose to us. It is the consequence of the facts, it is imposed on us from the outside, and in this prodigious linkage, which our world takes great pains to realize, the goals as such vanish; they are facts among other facts, but what matters is not the goal pursued, but the success, acting for the sake of acting, desiring for the sake of desiring. Pilate said to Jesus, "What is truth?" but Pilate did not need an answer to be an excellent Roman magistrate, repressing impartially all revolts, crucifying impartially all those who failed, dispatching with diligence the current affairs that had no value. Today we are all Pilate.

Thus, realism invites us to play a strange game. It sends us off in an infinite search for means, in an ever more prodigious development of what we can do. It persuades us that all means are good; it suffices to be the means to something in order to be right and valid. One can no longer even say that the end justifies the means, for within realism there is no longer an end; there is only the fact that the means succeed and that is all. But again, what does that mean? Simply that the means are effective, have an effect, no matter what effect. Icarus[8] was wrong and Blériot[9] right. Blériot did not have an end; he had the means to remain in the air. As for the ideal pursued, Icarus had it perhaps, to fly to heaven and to steal the secrets of the gods, but Blériot certainly did not.

Realism has, it seems, definitively blinded the enormous machine of our civilization. Everyone enthusiastically hails the fact of having passed one thousand kilometers per hour in an airplane. All right. But why? What is the goal pursued at that speed? There isn't one any longer, for one cannot speak of the greatness of the nation or of its security; tomorrow the adversary will go as fast. No, the end is of little importance; the simple fact of having reached 1,000 km. per hour suffices to itself, like all successes, like everything that is a "more," even if it is more of death.

Recently a politician said to me, concerning Joanovici:[10] "I don't see why Oustric was arrested; he was an excellent financier, and if he had been left alone he would have succeeded in stabilizing his whole system." Of course, he was arrested because he seemed not to have succeeded; what a mistake! [Given] six months more, he would have succeeded, and the success would have covered up all the fraud, the embezzlement, the illegal operations. Those who arrested him lacked realism.

Thus we are at the mercy of the limitless expansion of means

8. In the Greek myth, Icarus escaped from Crete by flying with wings made by his father, Daedalus, but he flew so high that the sun's heat melted the wax that fastened the wings, so he fell to his death in the sea.

9. Louis Blériot (1872-1936), French aeronautical engineer, was the first to fly across the English channel. This is an ironic comparison of mythology to Technique.

10. Oustric Joanovici was involved in a financial scandal in the 1930s.

for their own sake. We are at the mercy of the law of causality: we
have become its objects because we have given in to the great assault
of realism. It is no longer necessary to deliver judgment, [since] the
facts take charge, and we need only to follow the facts. This independent life of the means is what is the most striking, for that is
what renders vain all ideology and, finally, all politics.

For a new morality is born. A morality in which there is no
longer good and evil, just and unjust, legal and illegal, right and
wrong. This is a morality of what succeeds and of what does not
succeed, of what is useful and of what is not. And this is truly a
morality that today conditions all our life, and that is why it appears
absolutely ridiculous, in the face of this automatism of successful
means, to discuss doctrines or ideas. For there are not a hundred
means that will succeed in a given situation, since in proportion as
technological progress advances, the choice of means decreases; one
can truly determine in every case the best means, and when this
means has been found further discussion is useless. There can still
be dissensions between economic liberalism and [economic] planning (two means! nothing more) because the realm is technically
very complex and because technically exact solutions have not yet
been found, but it is thus, by the discovery of means, that this great
quarrel can be concluded, and not otherwise. Already, in all the
technical solutions, agreement is reached; there is no longer a choice
of means to exercise. In the name of what would one choose them,
[since] everyone agrees to take the means that succeeds the most?
To obtain the best output from a laborer, there are not ten techniques of work. There is one, and whether we be communist or
capitalist, planned or liberal [economy], one will make the laborer
work in the same way, for it is impossible to use an inferior means
when one is realist.

To balance the budget, the financial technique is also univocal,
and the most stupendous political theories change nothing. That is
why Hitlerism was led progressively to a financial policy well
known by all the classical financiers. To obtain certain psychological
responses from the masses, no choice is needed: the means of propaganda are measured exactly and people react psychologically as
surely as physiologically. Whatever might be the ideology that
colors this propaganda, it cannot be different, and that is why nazi

and communist journals are exactly interchangeable. This fusion of the means, this identity of the action whatever might be the thought, that is the great moral phenomenon of our times; that is what assures to realism a constant triumph.

No doubt, in the examples chosen, I have said: "to obtain . . . ," which then supposes a goal, an end. Actually no. For it is not truly an end that is sought, but only the application of a means. There is a linkage whereby the work of the laborer, the finances, [and] the psychological reaction are means, and whereby one employs the means to perfect these means, and whereby, inversely, they are not at the service of an end, but at the service of other forces that in turn are means, and so on, indefinitely. We live within an amalgam of means that no longer have any other meaning than to escalate and that tend to eliminate everything outside of themselves. That is the significance of political realism, of our new morality, universal and unchallenged. We are here in the presence of the fundamental prejudice of our epoch, as in other ages Christianity was itself also a prejudice.

*   *   *

In these notes obviously there can be no question of studying all the consequences of the political realism of which I have sought to lay out the components and the characteristics. I shall limit myself, then, to a few brief remarks; and first, a preliminary question that idealists clearly will raise. Cannot the fact of using identical means because they succeed be [morally] indifferent? Does that not leave the theory intact? Can there not still be independent political goals, above all that, in the service of which the means are placed? Does not communism or freedom or nazism create goals, independent of the means, goals well defined and sufficient to . . . justify the means, to return at least to the idea that the end justifies the means? Indeed, to this challenge it is exactly our study that furnishes the first response. [We have seen that,] despite their diverse appearances, all of the doctrines of our time are united at one point: they are all equally realist. They all seek equally to succeed and wish to employ the means that will succeed. Accordingly, they all obey the same morality and the same final criterion.

Now this morality is the morality of means.[11] Those [means] have taken on a preponderance such that they obviously overrule all theories: they have progressively been bent, sometimes in directions contrary to their intention, by the sole employment of means. For example, the fact that the masses are utilized in politics will be a decisive phenomenon; presently, to accede to power one has to have the support of the masses — that is, groups of people united arbitrarily by propaganda and by superficial sentiments artificially provoked. What characterizes the masses is a certain number of criteria: the criteria of artifice, of union by a mystique, of opposition (the masses are always oriented *against:* against the Jews, the bourgeois, the enemy, etc.), of the exclusion of all personal thought, of the fusion of lifestyles. Now all politics today is based on the masses and allows the utilization of the masses for every political act. It supposes, then, the creation of the masses as a political means: this simple tactical fact then implies the obligatory negation of humanism. The [initial] theory might be made entirely for humankind, but if, in order to apply it, one is obliged to create the masses, it becomes antihumanist. Thus neither in capitalism, nor in nazism, nor in communism, which all refer theoretically to the value of the person, can there be a real humanism because of the creation of the masses to which they appeal. This is one example of the very general character of our times: in politics, it is the means that count and that give to the theory its true limits. The proposed goal becomes absolutely vain and illusory because of the realism with which it will be obtained; that is why, in our times, political theories no longer have any importance, in any realm, neither private, nor intellectual, nor political. Lenin had understood this perfectly when he transformed Marxism into a method of thinking and reduced all communist policy to this prodigious tactical mechanism, which he described in detail.

Another consequence of political realism, in the political realm, is the petrification of the clash of imperialisms. From the simple

11. Ellul seems to be contradicting himself by calling what he criticizes a "morality of means" since he has declared that the goal of realism is to succeed. By this title Ellul intends to emphasize that since the *only* goal is success the focus must be on choosing the means that will be most efficient.

fact that there can no longer be any immediate triumph, in the most simplistic sense of the word, since everything becomes a test of strength, the political game is extraordinarily simplified. We need no longer burden ourselves with principles and doctrines; everything is replaced by a direct animal competition, a veritable "struggle for life." Consequently, there is a necessary political immobilization, since only those forces which are present are active, and since any internal modification of these forces would threaten to destroy the balance. It is no longer a matter, as modification, of adapting them in order to wage this struggle better. That is what was understood well by Richelieu,[12] for example, one of the first conscious political realists, who was to be the architect of natural borders and of European equilibrium. And, similarly, the theory of "marching with the stream of history" corresponds exactly with Marxist realism — since every force, every imperialism ought to be followed to the point of its extreme consequences, under penalty of ceasing to be realist. There is therefore no reason to be surprised by Russian imperialism: it is only the logical application of Marxist realism to a specific historical situation. There is no necessary opposition between Marxism and imperialism on the terrain of political realism. But obviously, the intrinsic development of imperialisms under this impulse, and without the possibility of modifying their character or limiting them (which would be contrary to realism), leads fatally to conflicts more and more vast between empires. These conflicts are no longer incidental events, ruptures of the peace, more or less accidental and avoidable; quite to the contrary, they are the normal consequences of a certain political posture common to all peoples. This contributes to transforming the relationships between war and society — but we shall examine this fact later. What is appropriate to note here instead is that all the meetings of politicians with a view to peace are based on realism; each one of them pursues its particular politics. This observation is very easy to prove, but one always has the impression that it is only an accident or [a result] of reciprocal ill will, when actually this posture is the fruit of a very clear political determination, realism. If indeed every peace confer-

12. Born Armand Jean du Plessis (1585-1642), French cardinal and statesman Richelieu served as the chief minister of Louis XIII (1624-42).

ence serves only to sharpen nationalisms [and] to reinforce imperialisms, ends only in bringing us closer to war, in yielding positions more and more mutually exclusive since there is no way to refer to any common superior principle, then it is possible to act only by virtue of a true sublimation of [self-]interest. This remarkable development, which transforms all peace efforts into causes of war, is a fruit of the implacable logic of political realism, which in effect, once released, pursues its own trajectory without taking account of contingencies; it develops according to its own laws. A beautiful example of this can be furnished by the Napoleonic wars. Even though the wars of the [previous French] monarchy or of the Revolution obeyed a definite political motivation and were part of general designs, one cannot fail to be surprised by the disproportion, under the [Napoleonic] Empire, between the enormity of the means invested (army, military genius, mobilization of the entire nation for war) and the absence of any general political plan. No doubt historians have done their utmost to discover political goals. But, actually, with Napoleon there are only impulses or creations *a posteriori*, in order to respond to a situation created by the war (like the Rhine Confederation[13] or the creation of new kingdoms). The true problem that we are observing here is precisely the consequent development of a realism that is an end in itself. The first Napoleonic war is the cause of all the others, each engendering the next, unfolding in the course of the development, without any valid reason except the necessity of Napoleonic realism. After one enemy there must necessarily be another, and to the degree that this particular realism supposes the elimination of barriers, it becomes urgent to destroy those enemies. An extraordinarily rigorous mechanism, which functions without goal and without end, for the simple reason that it has started running.

Now we have observed there some sporadic phenomena: Richelieu, Napoleon. Their realism, which so strongly marks each of their epochs, is nonetheless limited because it is tied to these politicians. It is not the posture of all the politicians of their times, nor

13. This was a grouping of German states under French protection organized by Napoleon in 1806 — which thereby abolished the Holy Roman Empire and brought about a new war with Prussia, whom Napoleon overwhelmed at Jena.

the widespread mentality of their epoch. Still, the consequences of this realism have been quite frightful. One cannot fail to be filled with fear when one considers that this same thought has [now] become common to all, to our epoch, and that this policy turns out to be supported consequently by the consent of all.

It is the same phenomenon that explains for us the remarkable political reversals we have been watching in recent years, in both interior and exterior politics (reversing of the alliances of Italy in 1915, of English politics in 1920, France in 1934-35, Russia in 1939 and 1941, America in 1945,[14] to take only some examples that are in everyone's memory, and in order not to yield to the notion that this would be, for example, a specifically German or communist machiavellianism); as of now, there is no longer any possible value attached to a treaty, a commitment, for the [only] measure of an alliance or of a political act is its utility. Thus no rule of law can be established in the international order, as Reves proposes (*The Anatomy of Peace*[15]), for the rule of law assumes adhesion to a superior value that measures and judges the action itself — that is, [in the rule of law] we are face-to-face with the opposite of political realism. The alliance, the contract, the League of Nations, the United Nations, international law — all of that is fine as long as personal and immediate political interests are not in play, as long as one has not found the path of efficacious political action. All the defections from the League of Nations, for example, resulted from the fact that a particular state had found its own personal mode of action and went beyond those limits that hindered its efficiency.

One cannot escape this dilemma: either one sets efficiency before everything, or else one sets before everything a goal, such as peace. But let us not be seduced by so-called solutions, [in which] one puts efficiency in the service of the goal, of the peace. That is only a verbal formula, for the means of efficiency, at this moment,

14. Italy changed alliances during World War I. When the Germans occupied the Ruhr valley in 1935, France did not object; Ellul believed later that opposition to Hitler in 1938 was too late, that it should have begun with this earlier occupation. Russia made a pact with Germany in 1939 and then broke it in 1941. The United States changed its isolationist position by joining World War II.

15. Emory Reves's *The Anatomy of Peace* (New York: Harper, 1945) was an early pro–United Nations publication by an American author.

will be limited, constricted, restrained, because of the goal itself, and one will no longer have truly efficient means. This dilemma is terrible, but it is important, if we want to understand what political realism is, to retain [the dilemma's] integrity.

It is quite evident that if this situation were clearly seen there would be general disapproval. But we must count on the lack of logic and of continuity in the minds of the crowds, with the result that the realistic politicians make their efforts to prevent people from seeing the true consequences of realism, and that is also part of this political posture. It is necessary to be a hypocrite. This is not merely the use of the lie, which was advocated by Hitler and is absolutely widespread as well in democratic regimes, but it is the practice of camouflaging realism under vague and noble ideas. The most realistic politicians, be it Hitler or Roosevelt, never failed to end their speeches by invoking the Almighty, which sounded absolutely false, but which added the note of idealism necessary for the elaboration of a purely realistic policy; this characteristic of hypocrisy is very strongly developed for this reason alone and not because of some kind of moralism: the cause of moral hypocrisy is the realism of action. Incidentally, one could note that realism of thought is such only because it does not lead to any action. Thus, existentialism is realist only because it results in nothing; if it becomes a realism in action, we can expect it to become as hypocritical as all the other political doctrines.

In the economic realm, political realism likewise represents an enormous corrupting power. One can say without error that all of the economic difficulties within which we are struggling find their origin in this primary attitude. On it, as a matter of fact, depend at once the organizations, the economic systems on which we blame all our troubles (which gives them too much credit!), and also the current mentality with regard to the economy. WHEN in the early nineteenth [century] the bourgeoisie created the capitalistic system by favoring the limitless development of industrial technology, the "progress" in every realm; WHEN "the necessities of capital" are presupposed as a fundamental given and everything is interpreted through this given — that for instance freedom becomes exclusively the "freedom of those who possess capital so that it can benefit them," and there is no conceivable freedom for the noncapitalist;

WHEN it is held that the productivity of capital is the first law and that everything else must flow from and depend on that, [THEN] one is acting as a realist, and it is rather on these bases that this regime has been built. Now the same is true for the socialist regime, which also subordinates everything to things, and which, for example, claims to attain an objective organization; it is a matter, then, of developing an administration of things, which appears to take the place of human government but actually turns control over to machines, to the necessities of production. It is a matter again of reaching equality by constraint, of reducing all human possibilities to a certain number of schemas provided for in advance, combined no doubt for human happiness, but which actually disregard the incommunicable part of humankind. Finally, it is a matter of the supremacy of one class, of the exclusive will of this class that will alone be considered, and people are no longer judged except by whether they belong to that class. This is exactly the type of realistic judgment.

Accordingly, without needing to develop further the consequences of this attitude for the economy, one perceives ultimately that the result of political realism in this realm is exactly the disappearance of the person. And that, whether it be liberal capitalism or Marxist socialism. In both hypotheses the real, concrete, living human being is crushed, for the sake of a phantom, whether that be the ideal economic human being of liberalism or the future communist person. This is the precise mark of all realism: the *Thing* comes before the human being. The law is the law of things, whatever these things might be, and one forgets people, unless one eliminates them in the elegant fashion of Marxist style: "There is no human nature; there is only a human condition," [as] I have already said: it suffices, then, to modify the elements of this condition, it suffices to act on the things that surround the person, and the person disappears in the combination. By whatever path, then, political realism leads to the annihilation of civilization and of humankind.

* * *

Finally, it is necessary to add one last trait of political realism, which is the characteristic of illusion in which people must be maintained.

I have already indicated that realism is necessarily hypocritical, since everyday persons would never accept this attitude if they saw and understood it clearly. To this idea is fastened the following verification: political realism declares, "Until now, all political attitudes have been unreal because they have always envisaged consequences and effects, because they have sought to palliate situations that were only superficial realities, whereas the concern is to point out the causes and to bring about a remedy for those causes." This attitude is very clear in what concerns the social problems: it is not a matter of mitigating poverty, but of modifying the social conditions that give rise to poverty and [then] it will disappear. And we must agree with this attitude, only its consequences are quite remarkable: given that this action upon the causes is very slow, that it takes very long, it brings about the following double phenomenon, directly implicated by the nature of realism:

(1) The remedy for the causes becomes a kind of ideal toward which we are *en route,* to which we sacrifice everything, and which permits us to tolerate the inhumanity of realism. Thus realism restores to the person what it had disavowed; it again asks people to accept present sacrifices, misery, and death in the name of an ideal society to be established (without any guarantee or certainty) in the future. It thus pushes people to live within an illusion, and here we have one of the most serious accusations we can address to political realism. Furthermore, it is hypocritical because it translates the true dissociation between those who manipulate this realism, who scarcely believe in the illusion, those who are its technicians and whom Burnhan called the Managers, and [on the other hand] all the other people who undergo this realism in the name of the illusion provoked by the search for remedies to act on the causes. We encounter in political realism as a true necessity (and I insist on the fact that this characteristic is the same, whether it be American realism, or technical realism, or communist realism) what has been, rightly, so much a reproach against the churches: a religion for the people, a religion as opiate for the people.

And this illusory character fits together perfectly with what I have said about the absence of ends within realism: there is not a real goal for action, but this action is accepted in the name of a paradise to come on earth, which would be an [authentic] end, if there were a scientific assurance of its coming, and if this action would mathematically assure us of its realization, which is perhaps what Marx claimed. At least, that is what was long believed about him. But Lenin explains extensively that the coming of paradise is not certain, and recent studies on the thought of Marx seem to confirm that. Ever since, it [has] no longer [been] anything but an illusion that establishes a little [more firmly] a certain kind of realism.

(2) On the other hand, this necessary delay in the mastery of the causes of disorder and of misfortune makes its analysis always lag behind. One begins with a realistic analysis of its causes [and moves] toward the search for remedies. But at the end of fifty years, other causes of disorder and misfortune have been added and a new analysis would be necessary: the old is left behind and it would be necessary to begin the search for other remedies! Thus realism is progressively revealed as incapable of following the movement of causes. Unceasingly, it is reduced to being only a superficial realism, and that is yet another illusory characteristic: it makes people believe it has grasped the [real] causes. But the people living on this certitude are deceived, because the profound realism[16] is left behind by events and is transformed immediately into a realism vagabonding in the midst of consequences.

*   *   *

What appears particularly serious at the end of this description is that there seems to be no way out. Today everything is rigorously realist. Our art and our literature confirm that. As I have already said, existentialism is only an epiphenomenon of political realism. But if everyone accepts this position, one can scarcely call it an ideology; if everyone considers it good and desirable (it suffices to

16. Notice that Ellul makes a distinction here by reclaiming the notion of real or authentic realism, which can claim in some verifiable way to be based on things as they actually are. Ellul contrasts this true realism both with "political realism" as an ideology and with a sloppy or "vagabond" use of the concept. In note 17 below Ellul will connect this distinction with the additional, "right" sense of the term as applied to Christian realism.

read the papers to know that this is the case), what solution [would be] possible? No turning back is possible. Now that we live realism, idealisms are left behind and recognized as empty. It is absolutely useless to resuscitate idealism, in whatever form it can be presented. It no longer gets a hearing from people. It no longer is at the level of the political and human problems of our times. Does it have a future? A prerequisite [for this] must be that the intellectuals mesh with the people. But [instead] present tendencies are broadening the rift.

It is likewise useless to place hope in a new moralism: neither a lay [that is, secular] morality nor a Christian morality will be able to change the course of our civilization, precisely because the sense of good and of evil has today been replaced by this realism, which itself accurately takes account of the situation of contemporary people. Where[, on what hook, could we] hang a morality today? Neither on facts, nor on humankind, for average persons respond perfectly to the use that technique makes of them. Say whatever we want about the eternal person, today it seems clear that with adequate means (and they are more and more perfected) one can modify the behavior and thoughts of people, sterilize them or polarize them. (There will, of course, always be exceptions, but as we know, today the exception is said to be the abnormal, which ought to be treated to become a "social" being.) People today are so well adapted to the machine and to political realism, and they will be more and more, that it is vain to hope for any reversal of people that would lead them to submit to some morality, a morality based on nothing. I know that this affirmation will shock [the reader] and that some will invoke conscience, nature, reason, etc. I do not wish to discuss abstractly: I restrict myself to noting that people today no longer have anything in common with people of the sixteenth century, for example, in their reality, and that they are perfectly adapted, from an intellectual and moral perspective, to the material exigencies of our civilization; that after a few years of well-done propaganda there are no longer two ideologies in a nation; that everyone believes in the same idols and that they are quite satisfied, if not with the effects, at least with the foundations of our society. No morality can reach this depth; for people in our time are not immoral, but only have a realist morality and by no means sense the need to change it.

Lastly it is, it seems to me, absolutely vain to believe that this enormous mechanism could be subordinated to a spiritual determination. I have already pointed out that political theories are determined, bent, [even] overturned by the power and the necessity of the means brought into operation by all of the branches of our civilization. To say as many Christians do: "It suffices to master these means spiritually, to put them in the service of faith" or again "It suffices to restore to them valid ends to pursue" is to prove great naïveté and a lack of true understanding of these means. One cannot avoid certain consequences of these means, and, among others, the fact that they swallow up all possible ends. One can no longer avoid the fact that [the means] have found a satisfactory ideal expression — realism — and that it will be a question of substituting for this realism another spiritual stance. But if we wish to proceed to this substitution we put in question the means themselves.

We are irresistibly driven to this dilemma: EITHER we accept the means that our society has created and we are then compulsorily realist, with all the consequences which that involves and which I have tried to underline, and if we want to add Christianity to this [picture], be assured that it will be nothing more than this hypocritical invocation veiling the realities to which we have become accustomed; OR we reject realism in the name of an authentic spiritual reality (which can be Christianity, but which can also be a [form of] humanism — the latter with all the weakness that is attached to human nature), but then one puts into question again the very means of our civilization, on which we are called to bring a spiritual judgment, essentially different from the judgment about success that realism imposes on our thought. We cannot escape this dilemma. We ought to be quite assured that we will not Christianize our civilization without putting into question again its very foundations and its *raisons d'être*.

*   *   *

The anti-Christianity of our civilization is not communism or Hitlerism, which are only ephemeral tendencies, momentary expressions; it is everyone's belief that is summarized in realism.

71

*   *   *

There remain still some misunderstandings to dispel. Anti-Christianity exists not at all because Christianity is a spiritualism, but on the contrary because [Christianity] is itself a realism,[17] but of another kind. Christianity teaches us first that we ought to see things as they really are. Not at all does it teach us to embellish or to interpret them; it does not push us to make a choice of what is good or true or elevated. It idealizes nothing; on the contrary, it invites people to pursue their apprenticeship, their experience, with the greatest possible veracity, lucidity, seriousness. The [concept of] Christianity often presented as an asceticism, as despising the things of this world, or as an ideal, an ostrich's consolation, has nothing to do with the Christianity that says on the one hand, "to the pure all things are pure," and on the other hand, "there is none righteous, not even one." Christian realism takes its source in some way in the affirmation of the state of total and irremediable sin in which human beings are plunged. If we refuse to see in that only a declaration of principle, if we are called to recognize it as a revelation, this revelation can have no other consequence than to make us discover what the world and we ourselves really are.

If psychoanalysis reveals to me the shameful and morbid motive of my actions, I shall not refuse that, for it only helps me to ac-

17. [Ellul's footnote:] In the study on Christian realism that is to follow, it will be quite evident that I am not taking a position in the philosophical or metaphysical debate. I have no competence in philosophy, and I understand nothing about the problem of realism and nominalism. I never speak of the Reality, of the essence, of being, of existence, of the Idea, etc., for I completely ignore what might be the question when these terms are used. I am thinking simply about the situation of everyday people, amidst their daily problems, be it their difficulty in providing for themselves or their apparent political decisions. Here I am considering only what everyday people call reality — that is, those phenomena about which their newspaper teaches them. Whether we wish it or not, the fact [is] that tens of millions of people consider these phenomena to be reality, in fact quite a living and valid reality. Political realism is related to that reality. The Christian realism of which I shall speak also has for its object that truth, which does not then exist "in itself" (as the philosophers perhaps might say, but I am not very sure!), but in relation to the political, social, and economic situation of people and to their beliefs about these situations.

knowledge, in a more concrete and material way, the judgment which God justly passes on my life. If the sociological study of our civilization brings me the demonstration of the catastrophe in which we are involved, that is only the actualization (necessary for me to take our situation seriously) of the fact that our world is the domain of the Prince of this world; if historical study leads me to deny the idea of progress and to observe that human beings are turning [in circles] in an infernal search for what can kill us spiritually and that the more we advance the more this happens, that responds exactly to the prophecy of Jesus Christ (Matt. 24–25) concerning the end of the times. It would be easy to multiply these examples, but it is necessary to indicate that this observation is not merely pessimistic; among the facts there are also valid, righteous, true elements that respond to the patience of God and to God's grace toward human beings. Consequently, Christianity pushes us to discover what is — in me, in my neighbor, in the world. Without deforming it and without judging it, because that which is corresponds exactly to what God reveals to us about our human situation and about God's action regarding it in the world. God by no means asks us to manipulate or to interpret the facts in order to make them accord with a so-called Christian doctrine. The evident proof of this is that God Himself does not at all conceal that he chose as bearers of his Word rather questionable people — for example, Jacob or Samson, and as ancestors of his Son an incestuous woman (Tamar) and a prostitute (Rahab).

Concrete reality must not frighten us; we must not veil it. Without any doubt, one of the causes of contemporary realism is the false moralism that was afraid of the facts and that had to be fought. And if this authentic, fundamental agreement between the revelation of God and the observations we ought to make does not take place, that is our fault — that is, either we have done our investigation badly, for example, by having confused a hypothesis for the truth or a statistic for a "fact," or we have listened badly to what God was saying to us and, for example, we have transformed the living Word of God into a doctrine and a measurement. The concordance between these two elements [God's revelation and our observations] is the central element of Christian realism. God does not separate us from reality; on the contrary, he plunges us into it, but that applies then to all of reality and not only to one of its fleeting dimensions. We thus discover not only material reality, but eternal reality in its unity, and not only spiritual reality, but living reality with its complexity.

An obvious objection then arises, under two different aspects. Some will say: "It is quite useless to proceed with this verification of facts, to know by human means what we find in humankind and society. Revelation is sufficient unto itself, and we shall learn nothing more than what God gives us. General affirmations drawn from Scripture suffice to know what our real situation is." Others will say: "It is quite useless to look for anything in this so-called revelation. The true problem of human beings and of society is in front of us. We should study it by our own means without trusting what others have been able to do, either because there has been no common measure among people of different times and places or because an eternal recommencement cannot be avoided. Anyhow, it is only the experience and the knowledge that flows from it that can illuminate us." These two attitudes seem to me equally false and, in any case, are not realism. It seems certain to me that the discovery of facts is necessary for the Christian, for it is the single thing that enables us to escape from abstraction. As long as I am content to affirm *in globo* that human beings are sinners, I do not know that I am one; only the law can convict me of my sins, yet it is necessary that I see them, that I confess them, and it is only then that I can take seriously the declaration that Jesus Christ died for the sins I commit, and this being put at the foot of the cross convinces me of my state of sin, going far beyond all experience and beyond the law, but that conviction is impossible without this first experience. And this reciprocity, each illuminating the other, can never be complete.

On the terrain of the political life, it is exactly the same phenomenon: theological affirmations are insufficient. They must be made real in a study of the facts, and that alone permits us to take seriously at the same time both Scripture and our situation. It is because biblical truths incarnate themselves that the Bible still appears as a revelation, and also that our human situation today is not mere folly, "sound and fury." But then this knowledge of the facts, this application [of truth] to the facts, this necessary experience leads

74

to the taking of a decisive position: because the world in its concrete reality appears (and only [appears]) as the domain of the Prince of this world, we are led to revolt. Not to refusal, which would be only an escape and ultimately a compromise, but indeed a revolt by the refusal to accept concrete reality as it is and by the necessity to tear the domination from this usurper. Such revolt is not at all spiritual, but perfectly inscribed in the facts. We have thus come to one of the essential characteristics of this Christian realism: it cannot be but revolutionary. Whereas political realism is necessarily conformist because its criterion is the unfolding of History, Christian realism is necessarily revolutionary (in the sense of changing the course of history) because its criterion is the lordship of Jesus Christ, which must be incarnated, when we never observe anything but the incarnation of the principality of Satan; concretely, moreover, we observe indeed that the deplorable conformism of Christians proceeds not from a lack of virtues or of courage, but from a lack of realism and from the abstractness of their spiritual life.

And nevertheless, how realistic the political attitude of the Judges and the Prophets!

Inversely, we should not stop with this necessary experience; does this not suffice to clarify our situation for us? Like the experience of grace, does not the experience of sin give us all that it is necessary [to know]? This attitude of many Christians cannot lead to a solution very different from existentialism. In the political world, what we discover can never be but a series of uncoordinated, inexplicable facts, and Camus[18] has reason to say that all human action is incoherent, absurd, in an incoherent and stupid world. Our experience, moreover, can reach only a certain extent, and not the true root of these phenomena. All that, however seriously carried out, still remains superficial. The seduction of Marxism is precisely that it seems today to offer an apparent explanation, but it is itself caught in the same interplay of phe-

---

18. Albert Camus (1913-1960), French author and winner of the Nobel Prize for Literature, is perhaps best known in the United States for his novel *The Plague*, published in 1948. Ellul, writing in 1947, is probably referring to his philosophical essay *The Myth of Sisyphus*, or his novel *The Stranger*, published in occupied France in 1942.

nomena. Human beings today severely resent both this incoherence and this superficiality.

Christianity does not offer an explanation that cannot certainly adhere with reality, nor an interpretation that will always appear artificial, but rather both an element of coherence and a view in depth. In other words, we do not at all lay over the establishment of facts a theory more or less Christian, edifying or not, but which in any case is alien to experience and would never satisfy us intellectually. On the contrary, we must first use the revelation that is given us to have a deeper, truer view of the phenomena than that which our experience, our senses, our reason alone can give us; on the whole, it is a new means of knowledge that God places at our disposal and that we have to employ concretely. Every simply rational or dialectic view leaves aside one important part of the facts: their spiritual tenor and meaning. Only the revelation of God can illuminate this background of history for us. But, besides, this revelation does more; it teaches us that the phenomena are never anything but the signs of another reality, of another existence. And it is that which gives both a sense and a coherence to these phenomena. Once again, this does not at all mean explaining them, but connecting them, because they are only the expression of a deeper reality that is revealed to us by God in Jesus Christ. Consequently, these political facts which we observe have a very much greater value than they could have to our human eyes, since, in place of locating an incoherent act within an incoherent history, we perceive the course of a more valid history, already achieved, already acted out, which channels, directs, and sometimes breaks the tumultuous, uncertain, but nevertheless irreversible flood of our human history. Christian realism is thus again at this point in total opposition to political realism, since it constantly seeks a reference to a reality other than itself. But this reference then leads to putting in place the political, economic, and social phenomena. And Scripture constantly invites us to effect this putting back in place. Indeed, one of the greatest present evils, with incalculable practical consequences, is usurpation. As a result of human usurpation of the divine throne, realism has led progressively to the usurpation of the premier places by all the material powers, and human beings find themselves dethroned, to the profit of the economy or of some technical application or another. Every power in the world seeks to usurp a place that is not its own, just as in the arts of today we see painting becoming magic, poetry becoming music, music becoming photography, etc. Now, political realism is in a way the orchestra maestro of this enormous confusion; it is what fosters all the aggressions, both economic and political as well as spiritual and cultural. The master of the demoniacal ballet reigning over a savant and technical incoherence with the consent of everyone. Christian realism teaches us, on the contrary, the existence of a definite order and leads to an effort to put [things] back in place. The model itself of this realism is the phrase of Jesus Christ: "all these things (economic goods) your Father knows that you have need of. . . . But seek first the kingdom of God and his righteousness, and all the rest will be given you, thrown into the bargain."[19]

This shows us precisely the attitude of Christian realism, which will consist, then, not in a negation of one or the other aspect of the creation (what both political realism and spiritualism do), but rather in placing observed phenomena in perspective in relation to revealed truth. This very phrase shows us also that Christian realism is essentially active. It will never be a matter of mere talk, but rather of an effort to penetrate into reality and to transform, modify the course of this reality. Therein we are really then in the presence of an authentic realism. The task is not to understand, but to change the world. This idea, which was developed by Karl Marx, was essentially, and well before Marx, a Christian idea, just as realism is found to be, well before our politics, a Christian attitude. But because Christians had relinquished it, others took possession of it.

*   *   *

I have attempted in this way to determine one of the characteristics of this Christian realism, and we have seen that, in these essential lines, it is in fact a realism, but that it involves consequences exactly opposed to the consequences of political realism. I will make the

19. Perhaps this last phrase, *par-dessus le marché*, is intended as an unreproducible French wordplay on *market*, which would refer to Ellul's parenthetical addition of "economic goods" in the previous line.

same observation with another characteristic of this realism: it is not static, but dynamic. Authentic Christianity has always been an anti-moralism, and therein it is at the same time a refusal to stand still and a realism. Moralism has the tendency to fix a scale of values and of judgment, and to conform the facts to this scale, to make all of life fit into this frame. But that is in no way Christian. The teaching of Jesus Christ, the fact that he came to seek sinners, for example (without rejecting for that the "others," if there are any), demonstrates precisely that Jesus Christ addresses himself to all of life, that he does not divide it into two parts. Separation will be the final act, but in the course of history there is no separation between good and evil (see the parable of the good grain and the weeds); it is the totality of facts, events, [and] phenomena that is received in faith. At no point does Jesus give us a rule to measure life. On the contrary, he announces to us the gift of the Holy Spirit, and it is only the Spirit who is our line of conduct: there is not a defined line of action, but quite to the contrary a quantity of possibilities opened for us by the Spirit. In other words, moralism is always a false realism when it tries to box us into a certain factual order and to define a certain mode of action; and Christianity is the inverse, for it opens to us all of life and frees us, following the Spirit, so that we can act in all possible ways. We have nothing to exclude in advance, since "*Everything* is yours, you are Christ's, and Christ is God's."

But this in no way means renouncing discernment — on the contrary. We need only to respect the difference between judgment (which we are incapable of pronouncing truly and which, when we pronounce it, is only an *a priori* that limits our action and the action even of the Holy Spirit) and the spiritual discernment to which we are invited by God and which expresses two attitudes: first, a choice that is made *hic et nunc*, under the leading of the Spirit, among the immense possibilities of our life, of our times, of our civilization, for example, and that is never a precedent; [and] second, awaiting God's judgment, which one can at no instant take abstractly and which determines our present discernment. Thus Christian realism, exactly because it is not a moralism, demands and presupposes spiritual discernment in the [midst of] the facts. That is what makes the link between the two elements which appear contradictory. On the one hand we saw the attitude of revolt engendered by realism; on the other we encounter (because we are speaking not of moralism, but in short of a gift made by God, of the world to Christ and to his Church) the acceptance of the world as it is (acceptance that is not an agreement). Everything that is in the world includes something of value, and everything is subjected to our discernment, which deals not with good or evil, but with the spirit who enlivens these things, [whether it be] the spirit of Satan or the Holy Spirit.

Consequently, in the face of the enormous proliferation of means in our world, we must proceed not by elimination — that is, not by a choice based on some *a priori*, not even the most excellent *a priori*, be it the human being or the spirit or the truth; one can absolutely not discriminate in advance what must be destroyed and what should be conserved. It is an illusion (for we do not have the means, and history does not advance according to our desires); it is an error from a Christian viewpoint. Nor is it any longer a matter of supposedly subordinating [the means] to the Spirit; we have seen how that is impossible. What is needed is to give back to these means an authentic end and to replace them in the perspective willed by God.[20] That also, and this concerns exactly this study, ruins the consensus of political realism, which is the demoniacal spirit of these enormous means, and that is what we must attack particularly, not in trying to favor some kind of idealism, but contrarily in affirming Christian realism by the thought and the life of the members of Christ. This leads to a fight to the death with the profound tendencies, but also with the detailed manifestations of our realistic civilization. We have to learn, in this battle against political realism, that no factor is indifferent and that the details are more important than the ideas. It is not a conflict of theories; it is a struggle of daily life engaged on the foundation of consciousness raising.

20. [Ellul's footnote:] On these two points, which I cannot develop here, see my forthcoming *Presence in the Modern World*, chapter 3. [Translator's note:] Published in French in 1948, this was published in English in 1951 as *The Presence of the Kingdom* and was reissued in a second edition in 1989 (Colorado Springs: Helmers & Howard).

Cartesian realism will say (but I am not a philosopher![21]) that one should consider as true everything that has been proven by reason; political realism, everything that succeeds in action; Christian realism, everything that conforms with the advance of the Holy Spirit actualizing the work of God as accomplished in Jesus Christ.

And all reality is included in this Christian realism, reality in its present existence and in its potential, for Christian realism here takes the exactly inverse step of political realism: the latter considers as valid only present success and releases to the future all the desires and the pain of human beings. For us, on the contrary, we can accept neither the one nor the other. What we take account of in the present, immediately, is the true situation of human beings, with their pains, their regrets, their hopes, their wills, without that being submitted to the hard sifting of events. We must, by faith, offer the entire answer, and all love, and all hope to people *hic et nunc*. We must refuse to give them the poison of illusions, false hopes, false remedies for the future. We must prevent people from consoling themselves by saying that tomorrow it will go better. We must locate them truly right where they are, in their totality, and consequently we must combat all the political or social theories that distill false consolations for people by promising them a perfect world in a thousand years. The Church has too much forgotten that we must not fling present concerns into heaven, but that Jesus Christ came precisely for all present concerns. And that the notion of the neighbor is exactly the inverse of [the abstract notion of] humanity.

Christian realism is an authentic realism because it refuses to take account of an abstraction and to work for an abstraction. Christianity knows nothing of Man (with a capital M), and Jesus Christ does not save humanity. He came to seek and to save each one of us who was lost, and for faith there exists only the people

21. Ellul says "I am absolutely not a philosopher" and goes on to describe his lack of interest in philosophical theologians and in Aristotle and Plato in *In Season, Out of Season: An Introduction to the Thought of Jacques Ellul Based on Interviews by Madeleine Garrigou-Lagrange,* trans. Lani K. Niles (San Francisco: Harper & Row, 1982), p. 16.

called especially by God for salvation and who by this calling receive their individualization. Christian political thought would in no way aim to improve the destiny of humanity, but simply to bring it about that one person becomes the neighbor of another. And this can be effected by two paths: on the one side, the individual, immediate path, which need not include material improvement, but which, by transforming the psychological or moral situation of a person, makes this proximity possible; [and] on the other hand, a collective path, which seeks for people (a few, or many, or all, but without surrendering to illusions about the future!) conditions of life such that the relation of neighbor to neighbor is no longer warped or rendered impossible by material conditions. But, in this work, what is the most important is to conserve clearly the immediate and urgent necessity of this relation. So that one can accept neither the sacrifice of this relationship [of neighbors] to secure it better in the future nor a material improvement of the human condition that would render this relationship more difficult.

It is this relationship of neighbor to neighbor that must be the present criterion of Christian realism, for the testimony and the value of the works of faith depend on that.

But at the same time that the Christian faith rejects hopes in progress and the relegation to the future of all present necessities, it also rejects the predominance of facts as criteria of action: for faith, the criterion for thought, for life, for action, for the good, for the right, for the true is the kingdom of God which is coming. The kingdom of God which is already present in our midst, but hidden, which appears to the eyes of faith only in the happy events of our life, but which stretches our existence out permanently. This [existence] is no longer abandoned to chance; it is no longer the product of a mixture of causes. It is, together with all the history of the world, stretched out, not toward an immobile and abstract end, but toward a power that is coming to meet us. Now, this kingdom of God is at the same time not only to come, independent of our will or of the course of history (since it is not a result of it), but also present and already real by virtue of the victory of Jesus Christ over all the powers that direct the course of history.

Consequently, because of this kingdom of God, we can never envisage political situations and facts as brute givens; we must envisage them in their development. Having renounced a biblical and eschatological theology about two centuries ago, the churches have always found themselves behind on the political and social terrain. They have quite generally taken account of facts, and they tried to respond to them. But by the time they had found a response, the historic situation had evolved and the response was one measure behind! So the church came to light as liberal when liberalism was already beating a retreat, and presently she calls herself socialist when socialism has been left behind by events. Among other examples! And it cannot be otherwise as long as one limits oneself to looking at the immediate situation without envisaging its development. Now, this [limitation], which is already an error for political and social thought, as Marx perfectly showed, is all the worse when the church does it, for it is an abandonment of her prophetic mission, [which is] necessary to maintain the world.

I hear well the reactions that such an affirmation will provoke: the church should not be prophetic about political things; she can be prophetic only in the proclamation of the gospel and for the glorious return of Christ. But that is [precisely] how what I have just written must be understood. And that is what will permit us to distinguish radically between two ways of envisaging political situations in their development, according to Christian faith or not. To say that for Christian realism one must consider, not a frozen reality, but the true development of political situations is not at all to say the same thing that it would mean for the Hegelian or the Marxist to envisage the future. For in those cases it is a matter of historic evolution, taking off from causes and following a process that may be dialectical or logical, while for the Christian it is a matter of an evolution that is inscribed in history, but that is metahistorical (in that it ends up beyond history), and taking off from an end that works, so to speak, in a recurrent way, in actuality. This end is at work already now, for it is not a goal, as [is the case] in all finalist [that is, end-defined] systems. It is a living force at work in history by virtue of the fact that Jesus Christ has died and risen, which is located at one moment in history; by the fact that he promised to be with us until the end of the world; by the fact that he is already now Lord of history; but [finally, by the fact] that all of that is sustained by the reality, to come, of the definitively established kingdom. Thus Christian realism leads to evaluating every political situation in its evolution relative to this kingdom of God, for every political situation necessarily locates itself relative to it, whether as a prophetic announcement, or as a Refusal (and one could almost use this word *refusal*, on the social level, in the sense in which psycho-analysts intend it on the psychological level). *And the genuine, concrete, historic development of a historic situation depends, not on a dialectical or logical process, but on this relationship, announced or refused, with the kingdom of God.* It is thus that the church must understand the reality of the world, and as long as she does not do this work, all her declarations and her works serve nothing.

All of this is nothing other than the observation that God, in his Word, addresses promises to us and that those promises which are present, real, determine in fact the contents of the evolution of the world, because their realization is absolutely certain. One can say, then, that the biblical foundation of this aspect of Christian realism is (outside of what is relative to the kingdom of God) entirely [the] promise of God addressed to human beings.

In summary, we see the radical opposition between these two realisms:

(1) For political realism, the final criterion is the fact, under its present aspect or even in its potential, in which case one will speak rather of history. For Christian realism, the criterion of action is the kingdom of God, which is at once present and to come. Thus, in one case, what judges human action is a variable and infrahuman greatness; in the other, it is a greatness of which the elements are revealed to us and suprahuman.

(2) For political realism, the problems of people, their misery and their suffering, will receive their solution in the future — a solution that one hopes [will be] perfect and absolute; for Christian realism we consider, not abstract humanity and the generations to come, but the neighbor, and we act *hic et nunc* to alleviate present suffering; solutions will consequently be fragmentary and relative, but addressed to the concrete person. It will not be a question of accepting the sacrifice of one generation, of a class, etc. to assure the happiness of others.

*   *   *

I have tried thus to determine what might be the mode of thought for a Christian in the political domain. This stance, which I believe to be the only one conformed to revelation, must be substituted both for moralism (founded on the past) and for the gratuitous affirmation of "ought to be": two errors that misperceive the profound biblical truth that every demand of God is joined to a promise. But still this kind of realism, as a political posture, seems to me to be the only door opened for a transformation of climate and of political thought. Only that will replace political realism, for only Jesus Christ could say: "I saw Satan fall from heaven as a bolt of lightning."

TRAJECTORIES

"Political Realism" is really an astonishing article — first of all, because in it Ellul combined *sociologie* with theology, two subjects that, for most of his career, he thoroughly divided into separate tracks. More important, in this piece can be found the roots of key ideas in a large number of his later works. In fact, almost every page of this article introduces a theme that is developed in one or more books.

Ellul's basic thesis that realism is a certain conception of the world with which we are all directly concerned (pp. 51-52) is developed in his major ethical work, *The Ethics of Freedom* (of which one section appeared first in English in 1976, while some of it appeared in French in 1973 and the rest in 1975). In *The Ethics of Freedom* Ellul elaborates the characteristics of political realism mentioned here, including skepticism (p. 53) and its submission to fact instead of truth (p. 54), but especially he presents to us the contrasting Christian realism in terms of the hope (not simply an emotion, but a present reality) that frees us to modify our thinking and conduct.

Though Ellul acknowledges in this article that political realism has valuable aspects, such as the coherence it establishes in the political problems of our times (p. 52), he insists that the realist solutions prove to be as fragile as others and not really solutions at all (p. 53), an idea expanded especially in *Living Faith: Belief and Doubt in a Perilous World* (1980/83). In that book an extended discussion between "Monos" and "Una" about contemporary society's confusions concerning solutions, reality, and belief sets the stage for Ellul's careful distinction between belief and faith, religion and revelation.

One especially extraordinary passage in "Political Realism" is Ellul's commentary on the loss of moral, philosophical, and scientific truth in modern society's radical relativism and submission to facts and technique (pp. 53-54). These comments, written in 1947, astutely prefigure our present society's move into postmodernism and give us some insight into why this development inevitably followed.

At scattered places in "Political Realism" (pp. 55, 62, 66-67, 76-77) Ellul writes about the loss of persons in the generalization of "humanity" and about the focus on utility and efficiency, themes expanded in *Métamorphose du bourgeois* (1967; not yet translated). The book stresses that the ideology of happiness (which veils a will-to-power) and

85

an emphasis on utility have become the predominant standards in Western society because of the all-encompassing character of the technological milieu. This leads to valuing things over human beings in the triumph of technique.

Ellul's related highlighting of the primacy of the economic over the political (p. 56) especially strikes me now, for I am writing this as the U.S. presidential primaries dominate the news. We certainly observe the triumph of the economic over the political in U.S. election campaigns, in which the size of the "war chest" often determines the winner — or even the possibility of entering the campaign in the first place.[1] When Ellul later picks up the theme of political realism in the economic domain representing an **enormously corrupted power** leading to the vanishing of the real person (pp. 66-67), he initiates ideas expanded in *Money and Power* (1954, 1979/1984). The book's biblical perspective distinguishes between wealth and Mammon and issues a radical call for Christian desacralizing of the latter. Thereby Ellul makes clear the underpinnings of his social criticism in his recognition of the contemporary functioning of the principalities and powers through money.

When Ellul claims that this power of political realism is no longer being discussed, but that it impregnates all the platitudes (pp. 56-57), he sets the stage for *A Critique of the New Commonplaces* (1966/68), which exposes the illusions of thirty-three commonly accepted sayings, such as "The Machine is a Neutral Object and Man is its Master" or "The End Justifies the Means." This book shows clearly how our society's platitudes serve as touchstones, as instruments of recognition, but thereby keep us from really discussing ideologies that dominate and harm us. For example, in the first chapter Ellul protests, "Let's face it, when television becomes a source of *Kultur* (a real culture medium, in fact!) . . . there is little room left for real revolt and serious consideration of human destiny." The commonplaces so generously propagated by

---

1. For an insider's perspective on this issue, see Bill Bradley, *Time Present, Time Past: A Memoir* (New York: Alfred A. Knopf, 1996). Also, Ellul's forewarning more than forty years ago that Technique would lead to major social losses and the loss of persons is confirmed by Bradley's recognition that the depressed wages and job insecurity now afflicting the middle class are due, not to job exportation to low-wage countries, but to the processes of corporation reengineering that accompany technological change.

the media "purely and simply reinforce the totalitarian character of the society in which we live."[2]

"Political Realism" expands the discussion of platitudes into the recognition that a morality of means necessitates the use of propaganda to arouse the support of the masses and that the journals of conflicting political systems are virtually interchangeable because they use the same means of ideological propaganda (pp. 60-62). Ellul justifies these claims in *Propaganda: The Formation of Men's Attitudes* (1962/65), which thoroughly describes the external and internal characteristics of propaganda, its categories, the conditions for its existence, its necessity, its effectiveness, and its psychological and sociopolitical effects.

The main message proclaimed by the platitudes and propaganda of the technological milieu is the importance of utility and efficiency and "more" (pp. 57-60). A critique of these values, of course, is the cornerstone of all of Ellul's major works on Technique. We can certainly see the accuracy of Ellul's prophecy that the "great quarrel" between "economic liberalism and [economic] planning (two means! nothing more)" — that is, between the U.S.A. and the U.S.S.R. — can be concluded only by the discovery of means (p. 60). After the downfall of the Soviet Union, many U.S. commentators seemed to gloat that capitalism had won — on the basis that the planned economy had obviously failed. Few were asking the deeper questions about the care of persons — a necessary set of questions with regard to goals, since in the meantime the gap between the rich and the poor in the U.S. had widened outrageously!

The next characteristic of political realism, the problem of the thriving of nationalisms dominated by the [spirit of power], which Ellul introduced early in "Political Realism" (pp. 55-56), is connected to the expanding power struggles of various imperialisms and the effects of their evolution on the relationship between war and society and on efforts toward peace (pp. 62-65). These critiques of nationalism, of (non-Christian) realism's criteria of success and utility, of the reduction of politics to imperialisms, and of the moral hypocrisy inherent in realism of action were all expanded especially in several of Ellul's later books, including *Autopsy of Revolution* (1969/71), which will be discussed

2. Jacques Ellul, *A Critique of the New Commonplaces*, trans. Helen Weaver (New York: Alfred A. Knopf, 1968), pp. 19 and 26.

below. *The New Demons* (1973/75) discusses the nation-state as the second "ordering phenomenon" of our society and criticizes the myths of history and progress that accompany it. That book's "Coda for Christians," in its criticism of Christian misunderstandings of the world, is a good model of the Christian realism for which Ellul calls in this article. *Violence: Reflections from a Christian Perspective* (1969) also criticizes misunderstandings — those that lead to Christian compromises with violence, the casuistry of just war theory, the conformity to the reigning spirit of power, and false types of revolution. The second half of the book issues Ellul's call for "Christian Realism in the Face of Violence."

A last characteristic of political realism is the trait of illusion (pp. 67-68), which Ellul thoroughly delineated in *The Political Illusion* (1965/67). This powerful book is especially important for our times because it exposes the illusions of popular participation, popular control of the government, and popular problem-solving in the realm of politics.

In his description of "Political Realism," Ellul only briefly mentions the arts (pp. 57, 69, 77). His recognition that they have been co-opted by realism and by the technological society and system is explained in *L'Empire du non-sens: L'Art et la société technicienne* (1980/not yet translated), which does not deal with art as a discipline, but reacts primarily to nonrepresentational painting and the school of art critics who proclaim its value. Ellul insists that artists, though they consider themselves revolutionary, are actually conformed to the system and correspond exactly to the character of the society they oppose. The book's critique parallels in significant ways Ellul's rebuke of the church in its conformity to its milieu.

Ellul's final point about political realism, which leads to the article's turn to Christian realism, is the recognition of the **power and necessity** of means in all the branches of civilization (p. 71). "Necessity" is Ellul's name for the order of the principalities and powers, as opposed to the authentic spiritual reality of freedom in Christ. This alternative he especially elaborates throughout *The Ethics of Freedom* and especially in the section on "Freedom in Relation to the Powers."

"Political Realism" shifts, then, to discuss Christian realism, best summarized in Ellul's statement that by means of it we "discover not only material reality, but eternal reality in its unity, and not only spiritual reality, but living reality with its complexity" (p. 74). Ellul's thorough description of Christian realism here (pp. 72-84) is a prelude to his second major theological book, *The Presence of the Kingdom* (1948/51), to which he refers in his second footnote (p. 79). This book especially reveals the importance of the concept of "the powers" in Ellul's thinking and the importance of the Christian life's battle against them, in all their materiality and complexity. Ellul explains his dialectical methods in terms of the image of the two cities to which Christians belong, a situation that calls them to plunge into social and political problems to modify the opposition between God's order and the world's disorder. Their actions to assess the social and political conditions with revelation as the starting point, to incarnate the will of God in actual institutions, and to watch ceaselessly to maintain God's order of preservation are necessarily revolutionary acts that must be guided by the Holy Spirit. To do these three tasks is to live eschatologically and not from an ethical **system.** (I have described this book at greater length because it so thoroughly expands the ideas of this article and because its call for a distinctive Christian lifestyle in corporate combat against the powers is the basis for all of Ellul's theological work.)

We must notice how often in "Political Realism" Ellul names the powers of evil. We have already observed references to the enormously corrupted power of political realism in the economic realm, the spirit of power in nationalisms, and the power and necessity that undergird all branches of civilization. In this article Ellul also writes that our world is the domain of the Prince of this world (pp. 73, 75); that genuine Christian realism snatches the domination from this usurper; that revolutionary Christianity incarnates the lordship of Jesus Christ in contradistinction to the principality of Satan (p. 75); that concrete phenomena are signs of the deeper reality of the powers (p. 76); that political realism is the master of the demonic ballet of economic, political, spiritual, and cultural aggressions — each power of the world seeking to usurp a place that is not its own (p. 77); that Christian freedom enables us to discern which spirit animates something — that of Satan or the Holy Spirit (pp. 78-79); that the purpose of his study is to help us ruin the consensus of political realism and attack especially the demonic spirit of these enormous means by affirming Christian realism through the thought and life of the members of Christ (pp. 79-80); that the kingdom of God is present and already real through the victory of Christ over all the powers that direct the course of history (p. 81). This recognition in 1947 of the important functioning of the powers of evil through social phenomena makes more clear the reason for Ellul's trenchant sociological descriptions of economics, politics, and the technological milieu.

When Ellul says that Christian realism cannot be but revolutionary (as opposed to the conformity of political realism and in the sense of changing the course of history) because its criterion is the lordship of Jesus Christ (p. 75), he broaches a significant theme that is elaborated in *Autopsy of Revolution* (1969/71). There Ellul shows how political "revolutions" indeed incarnate the principality of Satan, for those who revolt eventually fall to the same temptations as their predecessors. Political revolutions ultimately fail, because when they succeed they become like what they replaced. Throughout his writings Ellul calls for genuine revolution, which is possible only in relationship with Jesus Christ, who sets us free to be and to offer a genuine alternative to the spirit of power.

In his one-sentence paragraph underscoring the very realistic political attitude of the judges and prophets (p. 75), Ellul introduces a major theme of his book on II Kings, *The Politics of God and the Politics of Man* (1966/72), which depicts the biblical prophets as the ultimate realists in their objectively exact and rigorous proclamation of what God does and decides in relation to the political and economic necessities of Israel. Ellul also describes Qohelet (the Preacher) as a realist by means of the revelation of God in his *Reason for Being: A Meditation on Ecclesiastes* (1987/90).

Ellul's assertion that Christian realism is always an anti-moralism (p. 78) announces another main theme in his ethics, set out most thoroughly in *To Will and to Do: An Ethical Research for Christians* (1964/69). This book includes chapters on "Morality Is of the Order of the Fall" and "Morality Is of the Order of Necessity." Ellul insists that the radical freedom of following the Spirit cannot be reduced to an ethical system that thwarts genuine Christian life (a major motif also in *The Ethics of Freedom*). *The Presence of the Kingdom* (1948/51), footnoted in this article (p. 79), was Ellul's first major work stressing that ethics is not a system, but rather is a matter of following Christ and living eschatologically.

Ellul's brief comparison of Cartesian realism, political realism, and Christian realism (pp. 80-81) is perhaps his best summary in all of his works of what he means by those terms as he challenges Christians to keep the kingdom of God as the criterion of life and action (pp. 81-83). When he criticizes perspectives that look only "at the immediate situation without envisaging its development" as the church's "abandonment of her prophetic mission necessary to maintain the world," we see the motive for his own career in its constant effort to counteract that tendency. All commentators on Ellul recognize, even when they disagree with him, the prophetic insight of his work.

His final remark, that only Jesus Christ was able to say "I saw Satan fall from heaven as a bolt of lightning" (p. 84), underscores the importance of this article for readers today. We need Ellul's juxtaposition of Christian realism with political realism, of the life of the kingdom of God with the way of the demonic powers, defeated only in Christ. His insistence that Christian realism *must* be our perspective in order for our work to be of service shows us the reason for his own work — to try realistically to expose in social reality the working of the powers and to offer the alternative of Christian freedom.

CHAPTER 4

"On Christian Pessimism"

SOURCES

We have already seen from articles written in 1946 (Chapter 1, pp. 16-17) and 1947 (Chapter 3, p. 73) that Ellul was very conscious of the criticism that Christianity is pessimistic. No doubt it is significant that this piece wholly on the subject of Christian pessimism was published in the same year as the first French edition of *The Technological Society,* the French title of which literally means *Technique or the Stake of the Century,*[1] for Ellul himself wrote later that this book had frequently been criticized as being only pessimistic. To be critical of technology, when it offered "hope for the future" and "solutions to all our problems," seemed the height of folly and the depth of gloom. Sociologists in the United States initially thought that Ellul was unduly negative — but thirty years later they were asking themselves why they hadn't paid attention to his insightful perceptions.

Though it is out of order chronologically, this article seemed the logical one to follow Ellul's long essay on political and Christian realisms because it is Christian realism that prevents our social and human analysis from being merely pessimism. Perhaps some of us also have been criticized for what seems like pessimism when we have tried accurately to diagnose human ills in our age of false euphorias and vacuous utopias and hyped happinesses (including those in worship

1. By this title Ellul wanted readers clearly to see what is at stake in the world when it is given over to technique.

services). Christian realism is neither pessimistic nor optimistic because it is a genuine dialectic of total despair and eternal hope.

In this article as in the others I have translated Ellul's "l'homme" ("Man") with inclusive language, but that produces one problem particularly in this article: the transposition causes the text to lose the personalness that Ellul used. He would want us each to take seriously the state of our personal sinfulness, for example, and not escape into a plural humanity.

Since Ellul begins this article with a review of main points from the "Catechism," we should note some of his religious background. At age fourteen he received one year of catechism training, which he says "I did not find the least bit interesting" except for being struck by one passage in Pascal's *Pensées*. Ellul had had what he called a "violent conversion," which he never described because "we have heard too many conversion stories."[2] This conversion led to an internal struggle as he tried to flee from God in order to remain master of his own life. At age twenty-two, he read Romans 8 (see Chapter 5 below) and entered a second stage in his conversion. Reading Calvin's *Institutes* then led him into the Reformed Church, in which he remained active throughout his life in various capacities, which will be detailed in later chapters. It must be added here, however, that after reading Karl Barth, Ellul moved away in some respects from Calvin's theology.

2. Jacques Ellul, *In Season, Out of Season: An Introduction to the Thought of Jacques Ellul,* based on interviews with Madeleine Garrigou-Lagrange, trans. Lani K. Niles (San Francisco: Harper & Row, 1982), pp. 13-14.

On Christian Pessimism

Jacques Ellul

The various modern religions, such as nazism or communism, agree in considering Christianity to be pessimistic. Humanists join in this accusation, as do all people of action. Within Christianity, Catholicism easily accuses Protestantism of being pessimistic, and we have not forgotten the quarrel about the terms meant to characterize the Christian attitude opposite to action. "Active pessimism," de Rougemont said; "tragic optimism," Mounier responded.[1]

Christians, especially the Reformed, are in general very bothered when they are told that they are pessimists. In our times that is a defect — a sort of betrayal of humankind. For each one knows, since [the development of] the Coué method,[2] that the more harmful the circumstances are, the more it is necessary to declare oneself optimistic. The qualification of pessimistic engenders an obvious inferiority complex among young Christians, who seek above all else not to differentiate themselves from others, which means being optimistic, as the Americans and the communists are.

What is there of truth in this debate?

1. Denis de Rougement was a well-known Swiss Protestant author and philosopher. Emmanuel Mounier was the founder of the journal *Esprit* and the personalist movement, to which Ellul belonged until he and his best friend, Bernard Charbonneau, broke from Mounier in 1937. These phrases seem to characterize each man's thought.

2. Coué was a nineteenth-century pharmacist who developed a theory of healing based on auto-suggestion.

"Sur le Pessimisme Chrétien," *Foi et Vie* 52, 2 (March/April 1954): 164-80.

I. Catechism

We must begin with some data from the catechism. The first of these truths is that the world in which we live is that of the fall. This is constantly forgotten when we speak of the creation. We are no longer in the [original] state of the creation. That has been broken, has undergone a transformation so radical, so total, that we can no longer discern even by analogy what the creation was, on the basis of our world. [Now] it is exactly the passage to death of what was living.

The law of the world is the fall, the law of gravity. Sin has totally corrupted human beings, in their flesh and in their soul. They are incapable of doing the good by themselves. They can neither discern the will of God nor accomplish it. And every work of human beings is marked by this incapacity. Every human work is accomplished in sin, by sinful means, and manifests sin, which is revolt against God and is death. Of course, human beings have retained some practical reason, which enables them to act in the world and on it. This practical reason has existed in the measure in which it is independent of good and evil, and also in the measure in which there is a correspondence between the degradation of the world and the degradation of humankind. The means by which human beings can act on the world have remained valid when the two terms have deteriorated equally, [when they] have [each] been transferred into a totally different but respectively equivalent situation.

The second truth of the catechism is that this world of the fall is preserved by God in order that the work of God's love might be accomplished within it. It is ceaselessly held back at the brink of collapse and death by an act of God. God is ceaselessly present to this world and is at work there, with respect for human beings and with a view to saving them; although transcendent, God is constantly mixed into human history, and this is exactly the only positive reality of our world, a reality that depends solely on the freedom of God.

But in these conditions human beings are not purely passive. They are not alien to the work pursued by God, for God desires, freely, to join them to this work and calls them to intervene in it. That is rendered possible for human beings in that the cross of Jesus Christ has now been planted at the center of the world.

The third truth of the catechism is that the world cannot pass from death to life except by a transformation as radical as the first one. For the creation to be restored in its integrity, for the work that God has undertaken in this world of the fall to reach its fullness, there must be a mutation as total, as exhaustive as was the fall. We [have been] strictly unable ever since to imagine what that will be on the basis of what is. But what we do know, consequently, is that the present world, in the form in which we know it, is on the way to complete destruction and death. There can be no question of a progressive ascension of the world toward the kingdom of God, nor of a partial restoration of the world by God. This necessity for the world to go all the way to the end of the fall by terminating in annihilation, this necessity at the same time to pass by way of annihilation so that the work of God is accomplished, to which the book of Revelation testifies, is what has been called Christian catastrophism.

Finally, the last truth of the catechism to remember is that beyond this catastrophe there is a new creation. Therein the work of God and the work of human beings converge. For it is there that the work of the love of God is accomplished, for [the sake of] the glory of God and the life of human beings. But there also is accomplished all the history of humankind. Jesus Christ puts a stop to this history by *recapitulating* it.

This new creation is made in response to the constant desire of human beings, their demand, their plea, and God includes within it human inventions and initiatives. It is an *assumption* by God of human work through the Judgment.

But it is only at this point (which is situated beyond history) and only in this fashion (by a gratuitous act of God and not by a voluntary creation of human beings) that we find the conclusion of our history and the answer to our questions. Our work takes its meaning only by the act of the free grace of God, which adopts it and, by transforming it, inserts it into God's own creation.

*   *   *

It is around these elementary truths repeated a hundred times in the Bible that the discussion of Christian pessimism is played. From the outset they prompt two observations.

[First,] when psychoanalysts observe at the deepest level of the human being tendencies to sadism, the Oedipus complex, a morbid aggressivity, etc.; when they observe that it seems that [these tendencies] cannot be eliminated; when they observe that this is about all that one finds there in the depths (and not at all goodness, balance, etc.) — do we say that they are pessimistic?

When cyberneticians, applying and generalizing the second law of thermodynamics, observe that the world can only be going toward its destruction and its annihilation, when they affirm that the law of the world is entropy — that is, a mortal ossification, against which the points of resistance are ceaselessly threatened and in need of superhuman energy — do we say that they are pessimistic? The point is not to seek in these modern scientific observations a confirmation of Christian affirmations, but simply to note that when the savants say almost the same thing as the Christians, the savants are not accused of pessimism, whereas the Christians are.

The second observation concerns the rigorous balancing of the four points advanced above. Can it be called a system? No, for all this does not have any truth as a system. It [only] becomes true from the moment in which it expresses a living relationship with Jesus Christ, in which the reality lived by human beings is reflected, without which those affirmations are gratuitous.

Is it then a *consoling* system? For some, the response of God's love to sin and the response of the new creation to judgment are of the order of an unreal idealism. We can deny this, for those elements [of response] are not of the same nature. On the one hand, Christianity emphasizes factual observations with no way out, and to want to seek a human way out, to want to find some consolation, is then nothing other than a flight from reality. On the other hand, Christianity affirms gracious promises, without any present reality that can counterbalance the observation. These promises will become a truth going far beyond reality, and encompassing it, only at the time of a personal and direct relationship with the God who reveals himself. At that moment, the reality unveiled is bearable, despite the difficulty of living within it, but every objection to this reality of total sin and of death is at the same time an objection to the grace of God. This perspective therefore demands of human beings a renewed questioning of all that they are, of all that they do, according to the word of God addressed to them.

II. Consequences

If we try to extract from these elementary data a few consequences in the political or social realm, we shall unfortunately find ourselves at crosscurrents to most modern systems.

A first consequence is that sin corrupts every human social or political enterprise. If politics or economics were purely technical, human beings could succeed in them as in mathematics. But none of these enterprises is outside the framework of good and evil. They deal with human beings. They deal with the labor of people, their relationships, their appetites, their rivalries, and thus there can be no independence between politics or economics, on the one hand, and the choice of good and of evil, on the other. And when human beings pretend to establish a separation, they have in fact already chosen evil, and the simple possibility of choosing the good seems to them like an inadmissible obstacle.

Therefore, all political or economic works are sinful. The work cannot be better than its artisan. Sinful people can accomplish only sinful work, since this work is not done only by practical reason. This does not mean that people do not derive certain advantages from their enterprises. Evidently human beings succeed in obtaining what they seek. But at the same time, at the same instant, the consequences of sin unfold alongside this success, by the achievement of this same work. For example, human beings manage to eliminate disease, and this immediately leads to such a proliferation of the human race that, on the one hand, the dictatorial state becomes necessary and, on the other, the problem of increasing food resources is dramatically posed — [this] can scarcely be resolved despite utopianists like Castro.[3] This is but one schemati-

---

3. At the time Ellul was writing this, Fidel Castro was claiming that Marxism provided various kinds of agricultural wisdom that would feed all Cuba without Russian help. French news reports at the time characterized Castro as a revolutionary "idealistic and pure."

cally summarized example; I could cite a hundred. All human progress in political, economic, [and] social matters is paid for with an amount of suffering and evil at least as great as the benefit realized.

As for the highest human ambition to eliminate totally all human misery, disease, poverty, [and] war, we know that it is doomed to fail. For this ambition consists in wishing to re-create paradise. But Eden is guarded by the cherubim with flaming swords. Human beings have no chance of attaining it. Jesus announces for the end of time a multiplication of miseries and of wars. And the book of Revelation teaches us that all human history is made by the gallop of four horsemen. They represent the constants of history, which are War, Famine, Disease, and the Word of God. Human beings can do nothing to change these constants. All that they can do (and must do) is to brake this or that formidable consequence and labor to conserve the world, knowing that this [task] is truly the boulder of Sisyphus and that every breach closed announces the opening of another. Sin expresses itself in this failure to achieve the good, for it is not at all a matter of a purely moral good, of an interior good: it is a matter of the plain and entire reality of the good that human beings can realize. And how could we not believe that victory over disease or hunger is a good, when we rightly know that this disease and this hunger are the global consequences of global human sin?

We must therefore not retain any illusion concerning the efficacity of what we undertake. And the more [our efforts] seem to us to do the good, the more we ought to keep our spirit opened to the secondary or tertiary consequences that prove to be disastrous. Without that, we commit the sin of hypocrisy.

Of course there is yet one open, possible way![4] Human beings can succeed; they are straining today with all their forces to transform all human adventures and relationships into pure techniques. They would thus have the possibility of excluding all the consequences of sin. But beware of what that signifies. To eliminate all the consequences of sin means to eliminate human beings them-

---

4. I have added an exclamation point here since Ellul does not intend this sentence as a real affirmation, but as a hypothetical, rhetorical, ironic one.

selves, for sin is so deeply anchored in their flesh that nothing can separate them. If we pretend to do a work without it bearing the marks and the consequences of sin, that means that to our eyes the Incarnation of Jesus Christ was not necessary, and thus we put in doubt the death of Jesus Christ.

Perhaps, moreover, human beings will succeed in eliminating everything human — in reducing human beings to the level of a thing; at that moment their work will be without sin, like themselves, for the dead sin no longer. Perhaps that is the last match that is being engaged in before our eyes.

We ought not to retain any illusion concerning the future of humanity. What was yesterday will be tomorrow.

*   *   *

A second consequence, which normally follows the preceding affirmation, is that there is no human progress in the course of history, neither from a moral viewpoint, nor from a social viewpoint, nor from a spiritual viewpoint. Certainly, there exists some technical progress, but it is uniquely in this realm that there is any amelioration. In all the other realms of human activity there are some changes, some progressions (in the sense of evolution), but no veritable amelioration. And the judgments people have with regard to the past, apparently contradictory judgments, are to the contrary perfectly truthful.

On the one hand, it is true that the present is better than the past — this is accurate in every epoch — for in every period human beings have desired certain values, certain conveniences, have wanted to carry out certain jobs, and in general people have achieved the objectives they had fixed. What was their ideal of the moment could be realized, concretized. They obtained the object of their desires; they accomplished that which, twenty years or fifty years previously, they considered good. Accordingly, this observation, accurate in all the periods of history (and taking account that the fixed objective is eminently variable), explains how, from this point of view, one could regularly affirm that the present is better than the past.

On the other hand, it is no less accurate that the past was "the good old days." This idea that the past was better than the present is also found in all the epochs of history, and it is not at all a [mere] idea [floating] in the air, a myth, as Mr. Sacroy designates it with much levity. It is rigorously exact, for in every period human beings have indeed lost something — whether it be now just leisure time, now family stability, now glory, now virtue, etc. Everything depends on the point of view where one is placed. It is not an illusion to say that fifty years ago, from some viewpoint or other, human beings were better. Thus [people] judge [on the basis of] a certain value to which they are attached and which they see disappearing. Now, there is no doubting that in each epoch certain positive values from the past fade; only an unreal idealism would believe that human beings always accumulate without losing, or rather that the moral or social conquests, etc., of one epoch are transmitted to the next generation. In reality, at each generation, human beings gain on one scale and lose on another. What they acquire is paid for by what they no longer have. It is easy to observe this if, instead of judging according to narrow criteria and in a unilateral fashion, one tries to see the ensemble of the achievements and the values of a civilization.

Moreover, putting social or political progress into question is effected by the fact of technical progress itself. If we accept the judgment of Scripture according to which human beings are radically sinners and can do nothing good by themselves, that throws on technical progress a very special light. Technique gives people only the tools, but cannot at all guarantee to them their good use. Evil people will progressively do more evil, as their means are augmented. Now, human beings are evil. Technique develops indefinitely the possibilities of evil. And if we say that at the same time they develop the possibilities for good, I will grant that if you wish, but for that it would be necessary for people to be capable of the good. This actually explains why destructive techniques, and the negative effects of technique, are more developed than others; and it has always been thus.

But then this affirmation permits [our] radically rejecting the too-easy solution by which some tell us, "Technique is not evil in itself. Everything boils down to the human decision." Alas! No longer can we be content with the appeal to the "additional spirit,"

101

a leitmotif of all the idealists since Bergson.[5] There is never any chance that human beings will have an additional spirit, and if we recognize that this would be necessary to control technique, we recognize by the same [token] that there cannot be any authentic progress.

*　　*　　*

A third consequence of the data of the catechism cited at the outset can be named Christian realism. Indeed, only the observation at the same time of radical corruption and also of the efficacious love of God enables us to have complete realism toward human beings and society. One must be capable of looking at reality as it is, as black as it appears, without being frightened or scandalized by it, without taking refuge in ideologies, in false consolations. But equally, one must know how to discern every motif of hope and every gradual advance that brings us near to the kingdom of God.

Because it is encompassed in the love of God, the concrete reality of sin can be regarded face-to-face; because Jesus Christ has come into the world, incarnate in our flesh, we can stand our condition, however absurd it might be; because the hope of the resurrection is a reality, it is possible for us to consider and to accept the totality of the consequences of the evil that is in us and around us. Of course, these consequences are not theoretical or spiritual, but the most practical, from capitalist exploitation and bolshevik oppression to the lack of housing . . .

Now, the revelation in Christ is rigorously the only power that can give human beings the strength and the courage really to regard their true situation directly. *Every other* philosophical or religious attitude does not permit seeing this situation in its truth and its reality. Every other conception, if people wanted [to look at reality], would lead them to despair and to suicide, or else to refusal [to see], veiled behind an idealism or a justification. A typical specimen, in

---

5. French philosopher Henri Bergson (1859-1941) was attracted to the use of evolutionary data in philosophy and believed that intuition is a superior kind of knowledge, by means of which there is direct and immediate access to the nature of reality. He writes of both the spirit and the effete spirit.

102

the modern world, of this flight from reality by means of an idealism and a justification is furnished us by contemporary communism, which is the greatest present enterprise of mystification of the people with regard to themselves and their society. This mystification dissipates, moreover, as soon as one wants to look at the facts of the world as they are, and not through [the lens of] Marxist idealism. One of the first tasks of Christians in the world is consequently to take on the function of lucidity with regard to reality, at the same time that they take on this reality itself. Christians incur a terrible responsibility when they renounce this function, which they alone can perform, when they flee from social, political, and spiritual reality because their good and pious souls cannot stand the vision of evil. And who then will warn the people if not the sentinel whom God has chosen?

Christians have no right to fall into the snare of ideologies and of idealisms. At that moment they, too, become hypocrites. They must destroy these false consolations, these false hopes, first of all in themselves, but also in the world that surrounds them. They must struggle against religious idealisms (pietism, moralism) and philosophical idealisms; and in the realm of science, against the idealism of sociologists, of economists, of whom Fourastié[6] is a good example today. This rejection of idealisms will also lead, of course, to renouncing mystifications.

We encounter in the present world two kinds of mystification: on the one hand, those which provide people with a satisfying, simple explanation of the personal or collective situation in which they find themselves ("if everything is going wrong, it is because . . ."); on the other hand, those which provide people with a remedy, a solution, on which to center human activity, thanks to which their hopes are awakened and which enable them to be mobilized. "But," you will say, "that characterizes Christianity quite well! In what, then, is it a mystification?" There is mystification when the system proposed is a means of justification for the person to whom it is proposed, when the explanation and the remedy

---

6. Fourastié was an engineer in Jean Monnet's planning team. Monnet was a leader in mobilizing the huge Allied construction of planes, tanks, and ships for the war effort and later in establishing the first European Common Market.

enable the person to declare, "*Moi!* I am righteous. The evil is outside myself. I need not change myself, but must change the society or the others." When Christianity leads one to say that, then it, too, is a mystification. But in itself Christianity does not say that to any one of us, whereas every other system gives people this diversionary escape hatch. Christians have to destroy these explanations and these remedies because they prevent people from taking stock of reality, because they reassure people to their harm and engage them in evil adventures, because they give people a deceptive good conscience.

But it goes without saying that this combat against the mystifications is not negative. It can have its meaning and its value only if one provides at the same time a positive realism, the possibility of enduring it without despairing. It is not fitting to destroy purely and simply the systems that reassure people; it is quite necessary to give them an authentic reason to live — or at least to summon them to choose.

*　　*　　*

But on the other hand, this catechism assures us that Fate has been vanquished. That is the fourth consequence. If human beings are severely subjected to a bitter reality, nonetheless there is no fate exterior to themselves. The only fate, one might say, is that of sin.

Communists submit people to the fated dialectical march of History. Liberals to the fate of the laws. Scientists to the fate of numbers and of nature. They all disclose the secret of human life in fate. Christianity alone affirms that the human vocation is to redeem oneself from fate. The enchainment of sin is broken. The work of God in Jesus Christ is precisely to have broken fate, which henceforth can no longer carry that name for humankind. In Christ there is no longer either individual fate (for the will of God is not a fate; it is a relation of love, which is the opposite of fate) or collective fate (for God assumes at once the condition and the task of human beings).

Henceforth nothing on earth is irremediable, nothing is completed, closed, terminated: for Jesus Christ is in truth the remedy, and everything is promised at the recapitulation, which is the only completion, the crowning; until then everything is in movement, and people can never pretend to draw a line at the end of a chapter. No longer is anything irresistible. People need not yield before anything, for no law, no fact, has the last word. Material fact itself, even though the tendency of modern people is precisely to bow before it, is neither a proof nor a truth. When someone says, "It is a fact!" everyone accepts it, whereas in Jesus Christ we can respond, "So what?" Neither physical laws nor statistics are truths; they are aspects of the reality to which human beings are not at all called to submit.

Over against the entire modern world Christianity affirms the gigantic possibility that human beings, enchained in the fates painstakingly woven by society and science, might straighten up. The fact, the laws can be contradicted by people, for they are not called to submit to reality, but to have dominion over this reality, where it is the most rough and exacting.

Of course, there are constants, there are reasonable expectations, but history has not been written in advance so that it must unroll according to a necessary schema. Human beings are always called to intervene in the course of history, and their intervention can modify its course and circumstances, although it cannot change the work of God and its meaning. But then there are new circumstances, which God retrieves and integrates into this work of salvation.

Of course, too, this negation of fate does not take place automatically. It is not a human state, nor is it a situation. It is a combat in which human beings are engaged because of Jesus Christ. Only Jesus Christ has vanquished fate. And we can profit from this victory, which becomes our victory when we in turn engage in this combat. It is not fictitious, it is not unreal; it is a combat that demands all our strength, that must be waged without interruption, for the weight of fate, [albeit] conquered in Jesus Christ, is always ready to fall back on human beings, as soon as they separate themselves from their liberator. We are in the reign, not of independence, but of a freedom difficult to live, which is not an acquisition, and from which we benefit only if we accept without ceasing that everything — and first ourselves — is again in question.

*   *   *

This liberation from fate eliminates all fatalism on the part of Christians, and that is the final [fifth] consequence I would emphasize. The Christian position in the face of recognized reality is never a negativism, but on the contrary, because the reality is such as we have recognized, [our position is] a decision to intervene.

We must therefore participate in the works and in the enterprises of people — knowing that nothing definitive is at stake, but knowing also that it is within this participation that the incarnation of Jesus Christ and the liberation from fate can be rendered visible, tangible to those around us. Indeed, that is our vocation. It is necessary for the Word of God to be announced everywhere in the world. The white horse is also one of the components of history.

But we are responsible for its presence and for its path.

Christians should not develop any illusion in this participation. No illusion concerning the material usefulness of the common effort, since they know that ultimately there is no progress to be expected, in the sense in which [other] people hope. No illusion concerning the possibility of transforming individuals, of ameliorating them, for we should know that the only question that matters for them is that of their faith in Jesus Christ. Their moral or social behavior is of little weight. No illusion concerning the possibility of influencing institutions by Christianity. Jesus Christ did not come to bring a design for an ideal society, and it is a deceptive sentimentalism to believe in infusing love into economic or political institutions. No illusion, finally, concerning the possibility of making the kingdom of God come on the earth, by means of our reforms and our political or social activity.

Alas, I know the reaction of many Christians in the face of such statements. "But you discourage us! Why act under these conditions?" This attitude only proves an extreme attachment to earthly things, a lack of confidence in the action of Jesus Christ, and the intemperate taste, common to all our contemporaries, for illusions. Without illusions, they are confirmed as incapable of acting; to these Christians I will recommend only meditation on the parable of the unnecessary servant (Luke 17:10).

Being without illusion concerning the value and the efficacity of what our comrades are doing and of what we do with them, we can act according to the truth — and not before. And we cannot refuse this action, for two reasons. The first is obedience to the will of God, for God wants us to be among the workers of all orders, in the midst of and with the pagans, in order to be the presence of the Utterly Other at their side, the salt, the leaven, etc. If we love the will of God, this reason will already be sufficient by itself. But there is added to it [a second reason:] that we should participate in human works for the love of the neighbor (not of [generalized] humanity), and we find a neighbor only in this common work, this common search. The love of God has to be made manifest to people; that can happen only by means of the presence of those who have been the beneficiaries of that love. Now this encounter can take place in quite different conditions; this participation can adopt quite diverse forms. I am frightened that Christians today, convinced of the necessity of this participation, see only one aspect of it — *to do as the others;* to be in a labor union, in a party, in a profession, etc. — and too often participate in all the ideologies, the illusions, the compromises, which no longer can be called testifying to the truth, but should be called howling with the wolves, and whether these wolves be communist or bourgeois the point is the same. I believe it essential that Christians always maintain their reserve, their availability for other things, and that on the whole they might have a grand diversity of [kinds of] action. Where there is no questioning, where a frozen and blindered certainty reigns, there let Christians break the orthodoxies and be a living questioning. Where trouble reigns, despair and incessant questioning, there let them be the response of hope and of living love. Thus their participation can be of reinforcement, of concordance with the others, but also even of refusal, of rupture, of tearing apart. It can finally, alongside what all people do in common, affirm and elaborate an independent action, apparently alien to the present preoccupations, but nevertheless inscribed also in their history. It matters only that the Christian attitude not be theoretical, and that the incarnation not be a simple obedience to the sociological currents. Between these two extreme poles are located all the possibilities of a participation that is nothing but fidelity to the love of God incarnated.

III. Conclusion

I have attempted to circumscribe the contents of what is called pessimism in our thought. In truth, if God is not incarnated in Jesus Christ, if Jesus is not risen, if the love of God is not present in the world, if Christ is not the one who is, who was, and who is coming, then yes, our thought and attitude could be called pessimism. But it is necessary to comprehend equally well that if all of that is not true, then the NO that is opposed to human pride has no *raison d'être,* and, very simply, then our thought and our behavior *do not exist.* They are not pessimistic; they are nothing.

But if all these [Christian affirmations] are true, then it is not a matter of pessimism in all that I have just said. The terms *pessimism* and *optimism* are rigorously inadequate.[7]

Indeed, these terms imply two elements: they suppose adopting a subjective position in the face of events; in addition, they suppose an intellectual interpretation of things, which leads to an external judgment.

That is in fact the modern tendency with regard to Christianity, which is considered to be like a subjective truth, to be like a myth explicative of the world and of human beings. And to the extent to which it is one or the other, it falls in fact into the province of these categories of optimism or pessimism. This evaluation by non-Christians is, one must well recognize, often reinforced by the attitude of Christians themselves.

---

7. [Ellul's footnote:] That is why I consider Mounier's definition of Christian behavior, "tragic optimism," to be doubly inexact. First of all, it is not a matter of optimism. And in the second place, it is necessary to remember that the tragic consists in the human effort to escape from Fate: an enterprise in which the human being is vanquished. Now, we have seen precisely that there is not any tragic Christian, in that Fate is vanquished by Jesus Christ. [Translator's note:] With this reference to his opening paragraph Ellul positions himself against Mounier. Pastor Charles sees in Ellul's remarks a typical confrontation between French Protestantism and Catholicism represented on one side by de Rougement and on the other side by Mounier. Though this confrontation will be expressed more thoroughly in the article of Chapter 6, we must see here that Ellul, though Protestant, distinguishes his understanding from the pessimistic version of it represented by de Rougement.

[But] Christianity is neither a subjective position nor an explicative myth: it is belonging to the living person of Jesus Christ — that and nothing else. And if Jesus Christ is not the Son of God, and Living, then Christianity is nothing. But if he is, then it is a simple fact. If a stone falls, we do not say that it is optimistic or pessimistic. It is the same with belonging to Christ. That simply is everything. And the thought that results from it and the attitude that ensues from it are the consequences of a fact. Christianity then describes a situation, and this description is by no means optimistic nor pessimistic, for it is not an interpretation; it is reality as God sees it and reveals it to us, unveils it, makes us see it. It is a strictly objective phenomenon, and not a psychological, characterological, or sociological tendency.

Christianity, in the face of reality, poses an affirmation that is valid only for faith. But there again we are beyond the realm of pessimism or of optimism, for it is neither an idealistic consolation nor a rejection into the abyss of contradictions. It is simply the accession to an order of magnitude that can be assumed only by the relationship between God and human beings. And those who are outside of this relationship can only be silent, for [otherwise] they would be speaking of a fact that they ignore entirely.

And certainly, there is not any optimism at all where all possibility is denied for human beings to attain their own fulfillment themselves, but there is not any pessimism at all where Christ is victor.

But no demonstration can suffice; only life answers the accusations.

TRAJECTORIES

Though Jacques Ellul was not very interested in his catechetical training, his reading of Calvin's *Institutes* obviously had a great impact, for the foundational truths outlined in "On Christian Pessimism" appear in scattered places throughout all of Ellul's theological work, beginning with his first major book, *The Theological Foundation of Law* (1946/60). The first two truths listed in this article — of the fall and of God's preservation of humankind (p. 95) — are thoroughly expounded, for example, in *What I Believe* (1987/89). That book also has chapters on Ellul's views on annihilation/judgment and recapitulation (pp. 95-96 and 104-5), a theme he also explores in his biblical survey of *The Meaning of the City* (1975/70). The most thorough development of those points can be found in his *Apocalypse: The Book of Revelation* (1975/77), which studies that book, not by a verse-by-verse analysis, nor by a general reduction to a universal message, but by a thematic focusing on the movement of the book's structure and the resultant meaning. A chapter entitled "The Revelation of History" expounds Ellul's comments here that the four horsemen of the Apocalypse — representing war, famine, illness, and the Word of God — are constants of history which cannot be changed by human beings (p. 99).

Ellul's emphasis on the Word of God addressing the person (pp. 97-98) reveals especially his theological indebtedness to Barth and underscores a fundamental point in *The Humiliation of the Word* (1981/85), which challenges Christians in its last chapter to recover the truthful and incisive word (which we can speak because God's Word has been spoken to us) in a culture where the biblical "thrones, powers, and dominions" are manifested in "Money, State, and Technique." Not only does *Humiliation* elaborate the ways in which present society devaluates language through such aspects as excessive information (a specific result of the increasing technicization of society) and intellectual "logorrhea," but also the book criticizes Christians for their failures to speak the necessary Word of God, to defend the careful use of language, and to oppose both the imperialism and the covetousness that television's language inspires and also the closed discourse of ideological language. Ellul's challenge to believers to use language to "construct, exhort, and console" out of love for the neighbor certainly extends his rejection of a pessimistic view of Christianity by detailing more of the positive tasks of the faith.

I have summarized *The Humiliation of the Word* at such length because it develops so many of the themes in "On Christian Pessimism" — the way in which sin corrupts all social or political enterprises (p. 98); the fact that the Christian position with regard to reality is never a negativism, but rather a decision of intervention (p. 105); and, most important, Ellul's emphasis that it is the vocation of Christians to announce the Word of God in the world, his reminder that we are responsible for the presence of that Word and its course, and his warning against any illusions about that Word's effectiveness (p. 106).

When Ellul asserts as a second consequence of the catechetical truths that there is no true progress in the course of history — not spiritually, nor morally, nor socially (p. 100) — he raises the issue of the myth of progress, which he repudiates especially in *The New Demons* (1973/75), along with other mystifications that Ellul rejects in "On Christian Pessimism" (pp. 103-4). His comments in this article about the lack of technical progress, since technique gives only instruments but does not at all guarantee their good usage (p. 101), is a primary theme, of course, in all his works on the technological milieu.

We have already seen in Chapter 3 Ellul's work on Christian realism, which he names here as the third consequence of the catechetical truths (p. 102). His expansion in this article to emphasize the motif of hope and the slow advance of the kingdom of God (pp. 102, 104-5) is a foretaste of his book *Hope in Time of Abandonment* (1972/73), which first looks realistically at the "Symptoms and Impressions" of a world that has lost its way and then thoroughly describes characteristics of the present "Age of Abandonment." Then with equal thoroughness this book defines the genuine hope offered by faith and elaborates the theme of pessimism in relation to the freedom of the gospel.

Ellul ends his call for realism here with the question, "And who then will warn the people if not the sentinel whom God has chosen?" (p. 103). Ellul uses that biblical image of the watchman frequently to describe his own work and that of all Christians, most notably in *Violence: Reflections from a Christian Perspective* (1972/69), where he claims that we must interpret for society the meaning of events. That book, too, emphasizes the many forms of Christians' involvement of engagement and rupture and the need to resist social currents to participate faithfully in the world as the love of God incarnated (pp. 107-8).

111

Ellul's criticism of Christians who seem to participate instead by doing as others do, by becoming entangled in ideologies, illusions, and compromises that do not testify to the truth (p.107), anticipates two important books. *False Presence of the Kingdom* (1963/72) criticizes such conforming of the church to the modern world in Part One and then in Part Two rejects efforts to make the church political. Though Ellul ends that book with a chapter outlining the true tasks of Christians — their stance based on the revelation, their prophetic and reconciling ministries, their witness to God and their desacralization of society's false gods, their opening up of the world — he still recognizes that his remarks might be taken to be pessimistic. Yet he hoped that "[i]n this present night in which Christians assuredly are not fulfilling their role as the light of the world, God may not eventually make use of one or the other of these lines to strike a tiny spark."[1] *The Subversion of Christianity* (1984/86) expands these themes to review the failures of Christianity through history — concentrating especially on its submission to various principalities and powers. Ellul finds hope, however, because God is faithful, because "Christianity never carries the day decisively against Christ," because "the church is always the church of the living God."[2]

As Ellul insists, Christianity, as a life in relation to the living person of Jesus Christ, is subverted if we turn it either into pessimism that misses Christ as victor or into blind optimism based on possibilities of human accomplishment (p. 108). His closing reminder that no demonstration of this would suffice, that only the Christian life itself can respond to the accusations (p. 109), brings to my mind the haunting rebuke of Nietzsche that he would believe in a resurrected Christ if he saw more resurrected Christians walking around. This article asks each of us if our lives disprove the accusation of pessimism.

1. Jacques Ellul, *False Presence of the Kingdom*, trans. E. Edward Hopkins (New York: Seabury Press, 1972), p. 211.
2. Jacques Ellul, *The Subversion of Christianity*, trans. Geoffrey W. Bromiley (Grand Rapids: William B. Eerdmans, 1986), pp. 212 and 198.

CHAPTER 5

"The Meaning of Freedom According to Saint Paul"

SOURCES

In order to understand how Jacques Ellul studied and used the Scriptures, we must start with his own record of his intensive honoring of the Revelation. He described its beginning in this way:

> And one day, in a very explosive manner, it was revealed to me, very simply, through a text of the Bible, that if God does not exist, nothing does. I received that as a certitude that has never budged.[1]

After having found Marx insufficient for certain questions of life, Ellul found in the Bible a word that had not been invented or created by his own intelligence and that he recognized as being the truth. He asserted that "[f]rom that time on, my conception of the world and of human beings has been completely different."[2]

More specifically, Ellul declared that while reading Romans 8 he experienced for the first time a biblical text becoming God's Word for him. "Until that watershed experience," he explained,

---

1. Jacques Ellul, "L'Empire du sens, pour moi, c'est la Bible: une interview de Jacques Ellul," *France catholique-Ecclesia*, no. 1737 (March 28, 1980): 11.
2. Ellul, "L'Empire du sens," p. 11.

I'd never been *seized* by a written text. Never before had a text so suddenly transformed itself into Absolute Truth, . . . the answer to so many of the questions . . . a living contemporary Word, which I could no longer question.[3]

He found in that text many ideas that would characterize his future writing, such as the importance of freedom, solidarity in suffering, and hope in the salvation of the world. Ellul avowed that this text indirectly, without his awareness, inspired all of his research for the next fifty years.[4]

We will see in the following article how much the apostle Paul's proclamations of freedom in Christ influenced Ellul's readings of Scripture and his fundamental insights for ethics. First printed in 1951, this article lays the groundwork for much of Ellul's writing, as will be noted below.

Although in English we might vary the words *freedom* and *liberty*, French has only one word. Consequently, to be consistent I have used the word *freedom* whenever Ellul writes *liberté* and have used the English words "liberation" and "deliverance" when he uses terms related to *affranchissement*.

3. Jacques Ellul, "How I Discovered Hope," trans. Alfred Krass and Martine Wessel, *The Other Side*, whole no. 102 (March 1980): 28.
4. Ellul, "How I Discovered Hope," pp. 28-31.

The Meaning of Freedom According to Saint Paul

Jacques Ellul

Paul, when he elaborated his *"Evangelium de Christo,"* seems to have been the first to present the work of Christ for us as the liberation of slaves, and the Christian life as the life of liberated former slaves. And, in so doing, he was not taking up a simple image or a comparison, but he was intending to transmit to the Church the very reality of the Revelation and the action of God.

That it is Paul who furnishes this doctrine in the New Testament will be shown by a small statistical indication: there are about forty terms related to freedom and liberation in the epistles of Paul and eighteen in all the rest of the New Testament.

But this does not mean that Paul has there made an arbitrary creation, that it was a personal interpretation of Paul which could be doubted as an explanation of the work of Christ. Actually Paul is supported here, not by particular ideas, but by the entire traditional thought of the Jewish people and more exactly yet by all the action of God toward this Jewish people, as it is recounted in Scripture.

For, after all, of what do all the books of Moses as well as the prophets and the historical books speak? Actually just one thing, namely that the people who bear the promise and who have been chosen fall constantly into all [kinds of] enslavements and that constantly God delivers them.

Whether it was the political slavery in Egypt or in Babylon, whether it was enslavement by idols, whether it was enslavement

"La Sens de la Liberte chez Saint Paul," *Foi et Vie* 61, 3 (May/June 1962): 3-20. First published in *Paulus-Hellas-Oikumene: An Ecumenical Symposium* (Athens: L'Association Chrétienne d'Etudiants de Grèce, 1951), pp. 64-73.

by the law, whether it was finally enslavement by the state (I Sam. 8), this Jewish people whose first liberation ought to have been definitive never ceased to lose their freedom, and Jahweh never ceased to restore it to them.[1] Now, all this great movement cannot be reduced to simple historic events; the adventures, because they happen to the chosen people, have a prophetic meaning. And the Jews themselves know it well, when they consider the first liberation from Egypt as the pledge and the promise of all the others, when they give to this liberation a spiritual meaning (deliverance from the kingdom of evil), and when they look forward to a final and definitive liberation (Isa. 41).

Accordingly, when Paul shows Jesus Christ as the liberator, he recovers the entire scriptural thought; he shows that the action of God remains the same when it reaches out to the gentiles; he shows definitively that the prophecies have been accomplished by Jesus Christ on this level [i.e., concerning the gentiles] as on the others. He invents nothing of his own heart and manifests only the complete and radical results of these successive liberations.[2]

But this notion of freedom has often been confused and mixed with a metaphysical theory of freedom. That must not happen. Holy Scripture absolutely does not help us to resolve the problem of metaphysical freedom or determinism. It does not illuminate a situation of nature within which freedom would be included. It is not a question of freedom as such or of determinism as such — the human being is always placed before God; now, beginning the

---

1. Since the Holocaust, some scholars consider this particularly modern Protestant reading of the prophetic literature — that the Jews were *always* sinning and becoming slaves again — to be anti-Semitic. Let me assure the reader that Ellul was not, for he makes the same claims about all human beings — that we are in bondage to sin and cannot free ourselves. Protestant readers must separate carefully Martin Luther's insights into the apostle Paul's statements about human bondage to sin from Luther's later terrible writings about the Jews, which modern Lutheran denominations have formally renounced. The name *Ellul* is Jewish (it is the name of a month in the Hebrew calendar), and Jacques's mother might also have had Jewish ancestors.

2. We must ask why Ellul is so bothered, both here and earlier, to defend Paul against being original. Perhaps it is backlash against certain conclusions of higher criticism. Certainly it is also part of his lifelong endeavor to show the unity of the Bible, the continuity between the Hebrew Scriptures and the New Testament.

moment when human beings want to separate themselves from God, or they pretend to be like God, they have engaged themselves in the world of necessity, because God alone is freedom, and the freedom of Adam existed only by virtue of sharing in the freedom of God. Human beings are the slaves of sin. This enslavement includes, encompasses all the others, explains all the others. Political enslavement, economic alienation, servitude to passions, sociological necessity are only the forms, the expressions — aspects of that essential enslavement which is that of sin.

But if human beings find themselves slaves of sin (not fallible, but failed), with no personal possibility of escaping therefrom and of it being otherwise, then they are not free before God to choose on their own when God addresses them and when the gospel is addressed to them. To discuss at length the point that human beings as slaves of sin are *therefore* incapable of hearing the Word of God and that it is necessary *therefore* that they be [somehow made] free in order to choose freely, etc., seems to me to be absolutely vain; the problem of Christian freedom (in the biblical texts in any case!) is not located there, and the doctrine of Karl Barth on this point is perfectly illuminating and resolves this question very simply. At the moment when God speaks to human beings, this Word which is Love and freedom liberates them at the instant when it reaches them and places those human beings in a situation of liberation such that they can hear and receive this Word. Freedom is an ethical situation in Christian doctrine. It is not located at the moment when human beings would be called to choose their spiritual destiny, at the moment of a decision in the presence of the grace of God. At that moment human beings are thoroughly slaves. From the moment when they cannot be liberated from Satan, from sin, from death, but by Jesus Christ, they are still slaves when they have not yet received the grace that makes them participants in this life and this death.[3]

---

3. Even more than in the other texts of this book, the young Jacques Ellul in this article is a sloppy writer. This paragraph contains a proliferation of references to "this" and "those" that have more than one possible antecedent. Similarly, his continual use of "moment" is difficult to sort out, but all the latter uses are in contrast to the first — all other moments compared with the moment of God speaking. The next few paragraphs will clarify his intentions with this one.

And just as slaves can scarcely intervene in the bargaining that is proceeding between their Master and someone who wants to purchase them in order to liberate them, likewise with human beings toward God.

It is only after having been liberated, after the efficacious power of the holiness of Jesus Christ has acted upon them, that they begin to live in freedom. It is therefore not a question of a freedom of nature that would enable them to participate more or less in God's purposes. This idea is totally foreign to Paul. It is a question of a freedom that is counter to nature and that human beings receive because they are graced, and that enables them to lead a fully human life on earth, and to manifest on earth, among people, the power of God and the very freedom of God. For in the measure in which we are ambassadors of Christ, we have to "represent" him — that is, to show people his quality and his truth. And that cannot happen unless we ourselves live that quality and that truth.

Freedom is thus a problem of life, of the conduct of life according to Jesus Christ, as God himself lives in freedom. It is quite astonishing to observe, then, that the majority of studies on Christian ethics do not give to freedom the place that it should have.[4] Often Christian freedom is made one of the elements of the Christian life among others. And that [happens] even among perfectly faithful theologians, for instance in the ethics of [the German martyr to the Nazis, Dietrich] Bonhoëffer. Freedom is studied with the ensemble of "virtues" that represent the good. Other times one notes (Ramsey) that freedom leads to an ethic without rules, and one locates this freedom then only in relation to the old Jewish law.[5] But without doubt Paul goes very much farther than that.

He never cites freedom in the lists of virtues or of "fruits of the Spirit" that he frequently sets up. Freedom is not a part of the Christian life; it "is" the Christian life entirely.

4. Ellul was widely read in European and U.S. theological literature. David Gill reports that during his sabbatical in Bordeaux Ellul asked him, because there was so much literature, to prepare bibliographies of major U.S. ethicists so that he could read what was really the best.

5. It is noteworthy that in 1951 Ellul was already reading Paul Ramsey's *Basic Christian Ethics*, first published in 1950, in which the second chapter deals with "Christian Liberty: An Ethic without Rules."

Nor does Paul limit this ethical freedom to its relationship to Jewish law; it is not only from the law that Jesus Christ delivers us, but from every other lordship except that of Jesus Christ. Delivered from sin and from Satan, and therefore also from the law that was there only because of sin and Satan, we live in newness of life.

The liberation that is granted us must therefore reach all of the forms that the enslavement of sin could have taken on. It will therefore be a freedom with regard to the state (which does not at all imply a liberal state), with regard to labor (which no longer has the significance of constraint and penalty), with regard to money (it is in this liberation and because the Word of God reaches us that it is required of us to decide between Mammon and the Eternal), with regard to all sociological, political, familial conformities: that is, the necessities the world imposes on us. And it is then from that liberation that we can hear: "Do not be conformed to the present age . . ." (Rom. 12:2), for the present age is precisely that in which all the conformities are inscribed which the prince of this world imposes on us.

For we must recall without ceasing that the Lordship of Jesus Christ, the victory over Satan, does *not yet* usher us into the kingdom of God, that the world exists always as an evil power, that the world always has Satan for its prince. And that, consequently, human beings, while destined to resurrection and to pardon, are always subject to this prince — that the kingdom of heaven is in the midst of [the world] a humble, hidden seed, and that those who confess Jesus Christ are *alone* able to benefit henceforth from this liberation, in knowing that this situation of freedom in which they are placed is not an advantage and a privilege, but a responsibility and an extraordinary ethical difficulty.

The freedom that appears as a consequence of grace is neither one of the components of morality nor a posture that we can adopt or abandon at will.

Without this freedom, there is no Christian life. One can pile up justice, joy, perseverance, humility, truth, etc. If they are lived outside of freedom, [however,] that means that they are outside of the grace of Jesus Christ.

On one hand, freedom is the climate, the milieu within which all the Christian virtues are called to be developed, and without this climate these same virtues are not Christian: they remain the morality of the world.

On the other hand, freedom is one of two poles constitutive of this Christian life, the other being love. And all the unfolding of this ethic consists in a dialectical movement unceasingly renewed, going from freedom to love and from love to freedom. For there is no love without freedom, but also, as we shall see, no freedom is possible according to Christ without love.

It is at the same time [both] very simple and impossible to define this freedom. We know the celebrated phrase of Saint Augustine: "Love God and do what you want." This does seem to express correctly Paul's thought. Freedom is indeed the power that is given us to lead our life as we please. "Do what you want." And Paul answers repeatedly, "All is permitted" (I Cor. 6:12; 10:23). Precisely because the death of Christ tears us away from the fate of original sin, from the grasp of Satan upon us, from this interior possession by evil as a result of which not one of our acts, not one of our thoughts is good; precisely because now "[t]he Holy Spirit dwells in us," because "[i]t is no longer I who live, but Christ who lives in me," there is produced that extraordinary reversal which changes the very root of our being and which renders us free because now, when we act, we no longer express the Evil One but the Holy Spirit. Consequently we ourselves can choose our own acts, decide on our own what ought to be done; what we will do expresses the Holy Spirit. The moment the root is changed, the fruits that grow are also changed. As long as the tree is evil, the fruits are evil. Now, thanks to God's good will, the fruits are good.

And it is possible that the act be the same before and after, that materially our behavior appears identical: nonetheless it no longer expresses the same thing; it no longer has either the same origin or the same meaning. That is precisely why we no longer have to follow the law. The law imposed itself upon us as long as our actions, issuing from a heart possessed by the Devil, needed to be constrained, broken, repressed from the outside. The law was an aid to our good will in our struggle against evil, but this struggle was so ridiculous and vain. Actually, the law made more evident, to our eyes and before God, that our will was incapable, and that our acts, however controlled they might be, still sprang forth from a corrupt heart.

But beginning the moment that this heart is changed, the fruits it bears are no longer subject to the law. Without doubt those fruits which we bear freely, those decisions which ought to manifest the Holy Spirit, can still be judged by the world, by the moral laws and the philosophies, as evil and dangerous. This will even usually be the case, for there can be no possible agreement between the natural moralities of the world, which are necessarily bound moralities of obligation, and the morality of freedom that Paul teaches us.

He reminds us that the world can only "spy on this freedom" (Gal. 2:4), judge our acts according to the criteria that are not those of freedom, and condemn us precisely as immoral people. And in a certain sense that is true; the Christian life is an "amoral" life that recognizes no obligation to a moral [system], for in Christ we are indeed liberated from all obligation.

And in this sense, it is completely vain to elaborate a Christian morality; there is no Christian morality since, living according to the Spirit, each one is called to make her own decisions as her own responsibility. Each one has the initiative in the conduct of his life provided that it be in Christ. Why should anyone begin again to establish a law, precepts like "do not handle," "do not touch," etc. (Col. 2:20f.), when Christ has freed us precisely from the evil that these precepts pretended to make us avoid; they are truly useless.

We must be persuaded that there are no limits to this freedom, that the famous distinction "liberty is not license" has nothing Christian about it. Paul likewise says "everything is yours": we can use everything, for all is pure to the pure. We can do everything, for everything is permitted. And that does not come from a rejection of the law, from rebellion against God's order, but on the contrary from the fact that the law is written in our hearts of flesh, as had been prophesied about it, and from the reestablishment of God's order: the law is no longer exterior to us, and our acts no longer interfere with God's order, but they express the Lord's will and are found in accordance with the order. Delivered with regard to Satan, we no longer have to observe a morality. That invites us therefore to live the fullness of life and to reject all moralism, all asceticism, all mortification. There does not exist any "protected" realm where this freedom can bloom, leaving the rest

121

of life subject to the necessities; the freedom given by grace is not a spiritual freedom or an inner freedom. It is necessary that it reach all the realms of life, that it find a way to express the singularity of life in Christ. We have in all of Scripture and especially in the epistles of Paul an invitation to apply this freedom to everything ("all that your hand finds to do," says Ecclesiastes; "whether you eat or whether you drink . . . ," says Paul). There are no realms that are indifferent from the ethical point of view,[6] no situations on this side of or beyond slavery or freedom, for life is a unity. This freedom must thus be expressed not only in authentically free, and exemplary, political or sociological behaviors (and not in institutions) but also in worship, and even in theology. What freedom in any case commands is that we not lead a mediocre, petty, shrunken life without savor. Thus the Christian ethic is not comparable to any other. For if there are "moralities without either obligation or sanction," with the anarchists for example, they are based simply on an idealism, on the blind belief that human nature is good. Here, entirely to the contrary, this freedom is based upon a break with human nature.

*   *   *

But were we to remain at this point, we would not be at all faithful to the thought of Paul. He himself says, "I hold my body severely in subjection" (I Cor. 9:27) . . . , and we know well his great cry of despair which he utters in observing that he does the evil that he does not will and does not do the good that he would . . . (Rom. 7:19). Is it probable that he contradicts himself?

We also know those moral recommendations, those lists of virtues that he holds up after having affirmed total freedom. Is he going to reintroduce moral obligation, to construct a Christian ethic, which he so strongly denies elsewhere? Not at all. But what he means there is that this freedom is not indefinite. It is not freedom

---

6. Though many of the preceding paragraphs sound very Lutheran — for example, Ellul's explanation of the role of Law — here his words seem to point against the Lutheran doctrine of *adiaphora*, things that are neither commanded nor forbidden.

left to Buridan's ass.[7] It is not a matter of freedom without direction, without meaning, without orientation. This freedom must not be confused with pure fantasy, with incoherent arbitrariness, which would only be folly. This freedom expresses the action of the Holy Spirit; it testifies to the very freedom of God: it therefore has a direction, and we have to apply certain criteria to our free action.

Paul shows this in a particularly clear way in the First Epistle to the Corinthians (10:23-32). Our freedom has the goal of edification and usefulness. These two terms, which show us the true direction of freedom, must still be defined. And the following verses reveal to us what we should understand by them, when Paul tells us of the charity and the glory of God. Our actions should be chosen in freedom depending on whether they are useful for the charity and the glory of God; our actions should be chosen in freedom according to whether they build up our fellow saints and the Church of God.

"Usefulness" is not efficacity understood according to the world; it is what follows from "the body is for the Lord and the Lord for the body" (I Cor. 6:13). It is also "what contributes to the economy of God in faith — in a word, all that goes in the direction of accomplishing God's purpose for the world in Jesus Christ" (H. Roux, *Pastoral Epistles*).

And consequently we are extremely far from all the traditional ethical criteria. We are free exactly with regard to those criteria to choose by ourselves, to decide by ourselves what is useful and what edifies. We can therefore indeed be led to take actions that are apparently [both] contrary to the law of the Jews and also to the good according to the world and the philosophers, or again we can be led to take positions that seem contradictory at different moments, as we see in the very life of Paul, sometimes fleeing from the danger of death and sometimes encountering it deliberately. Indeed, sometimes what will be to the glory of God is eating or getting married, and other times it will be not eating or not marrying that

7. Jean Buridan was a fourteenth-century scholastic, rector of the University of Paris in 1327, who illustrated the freedom of indeterminacy or of indifference by imagining an ass that, being both hungry and thirsty and having water on one side and oats on the other, was free to decide which way to turn first.

will be to the glory of God. Not at all is there a common and universally valid rule for Christendom, and this is not merely because of exceptional vocations that set the law aside: all Christian life obeys an exceptional vocation. And reciprocally, the judgment that we encounter will not be an objective judgment of scales and statistics; this will be a judgment according to the law of freedom (James 2:12), but concerning this point I cannot go on and on [here].

When we act in freedom, therefore, we have to take the interest of others as the first consideration in the choice of our acts and our words. Freedom serves to express love for the neighbor. "Everything is permitted . . . , but do not seek your own interest; seek the interest of others." It is true first of all that love supposes such freedom of expression; it demands the invention of what can respond to the needs, to the sufferings, to the mediocrities of our neighbor. Now one cannot invent if one is not free, if one cannot freely use everything. And love is very poor if it must be inscribed within frameworks and laws. In this same text Paul shows us an example: we can use everything, eat everything, and in particular the "meat sacrificed to idols" (I Cor. 8:9), because we are freed from the idols' power. But if we see beside us persons who are perhaps not yet freed from this power or who fear it, or who do not yet understand the freedom that has been given them by Christ, then, in order not to scandalize them, in order not to give them a false idea of the Christian life, we should abstain from those meats. And it is the same problem, in political life, in all the forms of action: to be on the lookout not to scandalize the "little ones." For if our freedom shocks and scandalizes the powerful, those who have a solid and virulent bourgeois or communist morality, those who have intransigent precepts, those who are self-assured in their convictions or their authority, then we can rejoice in that; at that moment our freedom is very useful for them and, when we shake up their human certainties by our freedom, we do so by seeking the interests of these "others" (Eph. 3:10-11).

Thus, in the presence of others, our freedom consists in choosing, each time, by an ever new decision, by a constant invention, what can be profitable for them, what can be useful to them, what can edify them in Christ — that is, to build them up. Thus we must know what is the sign of such true freedom in our actions. Accordingly, these are not just acts of fantasy, but typical; and Paul, when he sets up his lists of virtues, gives the example of what such a usage of freedom can be. These examples must not return to being a law; they are not constraints, but serve to alert us and compensate for our apathy and our incapacity. Indeed, our freedom does not mean that the commandment of God no longer has any content! On the contrary. But because we have been liberated, what had been a juridical or moral law becomes a commandment of the Lord who frees us. The set of prescriptions, sometimes very detailed, that the Bible transmits to us should not be considered as without interest, without meaning. They remain before us as means of self-criticism, of an "examen of conscience"[8] of our freedom, for they properly signify behavior that is free with regard to the World; to accomplish them is to assert oneself free from the present age! Thus today they always give (not in their literalness, of course!) a concrete content to the service of God and to the love of the neighbor. Thus today they are always a sort of reference point by which we should unceasingly orient ourselves to restore direction to our freedom.

*   *   *

The other criterion of freedom in Saint Paul, [which is found] in the same text and which one finds again in the entirety of his thought, is the glory of God. "Do everything for the glory of God," he says, or again what comes back to the same thing, "glorious freedom of the children of God" (Rom. 8:21). Concerning this last text, it is necessary for us to note that it is not the freedom itself which is glorious — that would be only an image — nor moreover is it the glory of the children of God that is evoked, for the only glory is that of God himself; but these words rightly bind the notion of freedom tightly to that of glory. Now, we must remember that this glory is not a vague comparison. We always remain rather unsure when we hear this term, which evokes in us images of military or political triumph, in that the leaders are vested with insignia and participate in popular movements that raise them above the human condition, that make them more than human. But that

---

8. This is a technical term for monastic pastoral care.

is never what is going on in Scripture: the very precise notion of glory in John is found similarly in Paul. The glory of God is never a supplement added that would make God be more than God. Actually, the glory of God is his general revelation of what he is to the eyes of people. To glorify God is not to pronounce the words or to sing the hymns, but to show God in his truth and in his reality to the eyes of people. It is to testify about him, and to do so particularly by our life, in such a way that he appears clearly to people. (Correlatively let us remark that God never glorifies a person, nor can one glorify oneself, except in Jesus Christ, and when God glorifies Jesus Christ that always means likewise that he makes Jesus Christ appear as what he truly is — that is, his Son.)

Thus this freedom given to human beings in order to glorify God must serve to testify, in our life, about what this God is. I must clarify somewhat the content of this proposition.

That means in the first place that we must choose our acts in such a way that those who see them can find in them a reflection of God and learn by them to love God. That is the very meaning of the Corinthians passage, "Whether you eat, whether you drink (thus in the most material acts of life), do everything for the glory of God!"

And we see then how far we are away from an indeterminate, absurd freedom that permits everything. It is true that all is permitted, but before every undertaking (for which we know quite definitely that we shall be pardoned) we have to pose to ourselves the question: Is it for the glory of God?[9] Does it manifest God as he is to the eyes of people? This does not at all mean that we should pose the famous question (how famous and how false!): "What would Jesus do in my place?" Formulated with this naïveté, it now makes us smile. But there is always a present temptation, for example in the form of wanting to take on oneself all the Misery of the World, of tormenting oneself because of the hunger of two billion people, of pretending to combat injustice "in the long run": that is actually to pretend to put oneself in the place of Jesus Christ,

9. This is similar to Martin Luther's phrases, "Sin boldly, but believe more boldly still," or the Niebuhrian "right sin to commit." We must notice how oddly this changes the tone of the ethic of freedom that the result needs to be forgiven.

and it is in fact an alienation of our freedom. Much to the contrary, what testifies to another [person] of this glory of God is the freedom that is accorded me to be able to weep with those who weep, to share my bread with the hungry, to consider the interests of the other (and not first my own!), to do for the other what I expected for myself.

But there is also a deeper meaning; our freedom, thus received through Jesus Christ, is after all the very freedom of God toward his creation. But it is God's freedom in the measure in which we are God's children — that is, in communion with him — and consequently in the measure in which this freedom expresses God's will. And if that is how it is, we see well how this freedom can be to the glory of God. Indeed, the true use of this freedom, life in the freedom we have received, which is at the same time independence and availability, displays before people a quality of God himself, displays before people what is the action of God. Our freedom reflects the freedom of God; it witnesses for others to the independence and the availability of God; it makes not our acts, but our life itself into a reflection of the revelation.

And if our freedom is incarnated, be it in the most humble of our acts, then by that same act it witnesses to the glory of God, for it is called to manifest God's freedom on earth.

One understands then what burden this freedom can represent, if, living freely, we are obliged to ask ourselves: as a free person, am I witnessing to the freedom of God? In the face of this responsibility, one understands the frightened retreat of those who prefer to reconstruct a law, a morality, a code. The Puritans, like the Catholics, retreated from the test of Christian freedom; once started in this adventure, we no longer have any possible tranquility, nor a good conscience, nor justification. Free, most certainly, but because conscious of this responsibility, we do everything (for everything is permitted) in the knowledge that our freedom will never be to the measure of the One who gives it to us; we have no other recourse than to hand back to him the unworthy fruits of this glorious freedom in order for him to forgive them, for in the exercise of this freedom everything depends on God: freedom is never "ours."

Thus, making use of everything (as not making use of it), profiting from everything (for everything is ours), we know well that it is to the glory of God only *if* we are pure (to the pure everything is pure — but my being purified depends on the grace of God), only *if* we belong to Christ (everything belongs to you, you belong to Christ). And *we* can never have a good conscience in using this freedom, yet we cannot live otherwise in order to be faithful except in this freedom, this gratuitousness, this availability, for it is to this freedom that we have been called by Christ, and it is in order to testify to the glory of God that we have been chosen.

*   *   *

Paul constantly renews the recommendation: Do not become slaves again (I Cor. 6:12; 7:23).

There is one form of this slavery to which we have just alluded: so-called Christian morality.

When we try to make more precise the rules of the Christian life, to construct a moral code, a model that must be imitated and accomplished, we betray Jesus Christ himself. We despise this freedom that he acquired for us with such difficulty by his death; we fall back into the old enslavements, and we repudiate the title of children of God.

The Christian life is not a moral life, precisely because it does not obey a law, but it belongs to Christ, it is in communion with the will of God, and this will is not Law, but Love and Freedom.

One can also lose the freedom that is accorded us by grace by reintroducing into our life some other lord, by our submission to the Spirit of the World, which is always possible, and of which the epistles of Paul (especially the pastorals) give several examples. We alienate this freedom when we commit ourselves to a sociological current, to a social conformism, in pretending that it is the manifestation of the Christian life (e.g., the political conformism founded on a Christian political doctrine, adhesion to an economic system as an expression of the revealed truth or of love, etc.), each time that we justify with Christian motivations, for example, one of our political attitudes (almost always taken for motives of sociology or passions): we thereby cease to be free in Christ.

It is the same when we think we can entrust ourselves to an objective system in order to assure "the" freedom of human beings:

when we think that political or economic institutions will give freedom to people and will render them free, when we consider *that the obstacle to human freedom* is, for example, one [particular] authoritarian form of the State or economic alienation, then we ourselves lose our freedom.

It is the same when we pretend to regain human freedom by a philosophy of Nature or of Being. As soon as we seek to ensure, explain, demonstrate this freedom on the basis of a system, that means that we necessarily abandon Jesus Christ and his liberating action, eternal and present. Among a hundred examples we may point out that the system of Teilhard de Chardin is today certainly the most efficacious intellectual means of alienating the freedom acquired in Christ. It is one of the most dangerous anti-Christian enterprises of our days because of its pseudo-demonstration of the accomplishment of the cosmic (?) Christ by a sort of necessity intrinsic to nature, because of its volatilization of the Incarnation, and because of its confusion between freedom and historical necessity. We could multiply the examples!

But we must go farther; when we begin with this double orientation of freedom, which for Paul is charity and glory, we immediately encounter the possibility of a serious confusion: one can think in fact that it is a matter of finding the "good use of freedom" and that Paul would show us that good use, whereas if we did not take account of these elements we would make a bad use of it. I believe that this interpretation is completely inaccurate. Paul actually goes much farther: if we live in charity and for the glory [of God] we are in freedom; otherwise freedom does not exist. It is therefore not a question of the usage of freedom, but of its very existence.

There is no freedom without love. This freedom centered on the desire of human beings, on their spirit of power, on their personality, is exactly one of the forms of this new slavery of which Paul speaks: "Everything is permitted me, but I will not let myself be enslaved by anything . . ." (I Cor. 6:12), and as an example of this freedom without love which is only slavery he accurately cites the union of a man with a prostitute — that is, precisely the example in which a man uses his freedom while despising a creature of God . . .

It is like this because we are not freed except by the love of God, and because if we place ourselves outside of love we place ourselves outside of this freedom that comes from the God of Love. Without doubt it would be possible to demonstrate the ontological link between freedom and love, but it is more fitting, since Paul did not do it, to consider here only the theological link between the two.

There is no freedom except by the new relation that God establishes among beings, for in the old relation according to the world, with its connections of force, violence, and subjection, there could not be any kind of freedom, as we have in fact observed. Now, in the measure of this new relation, freedom is established for the choice of our behavior and for the direction of our life (as a consequence with regard to Satan and the Law), but this new relation is precisely that of love, which teaches us to seek the interests of others.

There is not more freedom when our life is not to the glory of God. Indeed, we would have to believe in freedom as such, in a freedom existing by itself, like what the revolutionaries of 1789 promised. But we well know that such freedom in itself does not exist in any form. To take the terms of Roman law, we are not "Ingenui" but "Libertini," not people free by nature and by birth but the liberated who receive freedom from their masters. And this freedom never exists by itself; it exists only with respect to the gift of God, only as an expression of the very freedom of God, as we already said, and actually *guaranteed by* God's freedom. If our freedom were not guaranteed in a true relationship between creatures and their creator, which has been restored in Jesus Christ alone, then it would cease to be. That is how we should understand the distinction between the free person (which we are not) and the freed person (which we will never cease to be). It is at each new stage that God always liberates us afresh. He does not introduce us into a permanent, durable state, an accomplished situation, but rather into a mode of being-with-him. If we pretended to the status of free people, our freedom would cease to reflect that of God, to be in relation with that of God, and would thereby cease radically to exist. If, to the contrary, we accept this mode of being that God chooses for us, then our freedom, always new, always young, ceaselessly points to the One who renews it.

That means that our freedom is not consumed by the effort to manage our life, in the intellectual or political choices we have to

130

make; it extends much farther, it refers back to a higher freedom, it holds its value only in the measure to which it is the sign of the very freedom of God. Without that, it points nowhere, it empties into the void; it is a freedom without meaning.

But to reflect the freedom of God is to exist rightly for the glory of God. And when we refuse that, then we seek to grasp for ourselves what does not belong to us, we cut our freedom off from its root, and as a result of wanting [freedom] "in itself" we see it drying up and withering in our lives. We submit — subordinate ourselves, as a matter of fact — to our search for glory and power, which renders us slaves of the powers of this world, from which Christ delivered us.

Watch, then, lest you lose this freedom, Paul often reminds us; we lose it when we separate it from the charity and the glory of God. Here exhortation necessarily merges with theology. Why after all would we not risk *also* this freedom in the game of life? Because, Paul answers, you have been redeemed at great price. And when we consider indeed the price that has been paid by God to redeem us, then we become ashamed at the very idea that we might risk this freedom, which becomes the most precious value of our life.

TRAJECTORIES

This early biblical article, written in 1951, is foundational for much of Ellul's study of the Scriptures and his ethics. In his initial insistence that Paul invented nothing new, but rather built upon the Jewish Scriptures (pp. 115-16), we find the roots of his lifelong insistence on the unity of the Revelation. This sense of continuity undergirds *The Meaning of the City* (1975/70), which traces that theme through the whole Bible. Sometimes, however, Ellul organizes that unity so christocentrically, rather than as a progression of Revelation first to the Jews and then through Christ, that he does not honor the Hebrew Scriptures as texts with meanings in their own time. That is especially a problem in *The Judgment of Jonah,* published shortly after this article (1952/71).

Ellul's rejection in this article of attempts to make the Scriptures solve the problems of metaphysics or determinism and his declaration instead that the question is one of humankind situated before God (p. 116) are both developed in sections of *The Ethics of Freedom* (1973, 1975/1976). There he also elaborates his description here of how human beings are slaves to sin (p. 117), which makes clear the theological import of many of the ideas developed in Ellul's sociological works. By specifically rooting the world of social necessity (a theme repeated here also on pp. 118, 121, and 129) in the sin of humankind, by recognizing political and economic bondages as only the forms of the slavery of sin, Ellul connects his sociological assessments of those bondages with the theological concepts of sin and of the principalities and powers.

As is evidenced throughout his theological works, Ellul follows Karl Barth precisely in the idea that, in the moment when God speaks to the individual, the Word frees the person at the instant of hearing and puts him or her in a situation of liberation so that the Word can be heard further and received (p. 117). This gives rise to Ellul's complaint that ethics books don't give freedom its proper place — that of the situation of relationship with God rather than as one of the virtues or spiritual gifts (p. 118) — a deficiency Ellul himself remedied in *The Ethics of Freedom*.

It must be noticed that Ellul's description of freedom (pp. 118-21, 129-30), both here and as a primary focus in *The Ethics*, means freedom from the powers. Ellul groups together in this list sin, Satan (or the Evil One, the Devil, or the prince of this world), and various kinds of lordships such as the State or Mammon — entities elsewhere called powers — as the forces from which we are freed.

The argument that freedom is the milieu for Christians (pp. 120-21) contrasts with Ellul's constant sociological arguments against technology as the threatening milieu of our age. Scattered throughout his theological works are comments that Christians can observe the technological society more truly and address it more prophetically because they are based in an alternative milieu.

Ellul's rejection of moralities and his plea to recognize Christian ethics rather as amoral (pp. 121-22) are themes he developed in *To Will and to Do: An Ethical Research for Christians* (1964/69). That book does not so much reject the possibility of Christian ethics as object to the legislation of ethics demanding a morality of law rather than offering guidance in the freedom of the gospel. The verse from Ecclesiastes that Ellul cites to illustrate this point in the article is wonderfully explicated in *Reason for Being: A Meditation on Ecclesiastes* (1987/90).

When Ellul indicts the idealism of the anarchists' "moralities without either obligation or sanction" as being based "on the blind belief that human nature is good" (p. 122), he is referring to ideological anarchism. In his later book *Anarchy and Christianity* (1988/91), he similarly rejects this type of anarchy in favor of the genuine anarchy of following Christ. His indebtedness to Kierkegaard is notable in this book in his strong reproach of Christendom and his call for genuine *Christian* faith.

This article's careful distinction between reintroducing obligations and signifying that this freedom is not indeterminate or without direction (p. 123) is an important one for Ellul's *Ethics,* in which the final chapter sketches concrete implications of his understanding of freedom. There Ellul addresses issues of politics, religion, family, work, sex, money, and vocation and models an application of the criteria of edification and "usefulness" (not as efficiency, but as it contributes to the economy of God) as directions for expressing the action of the Holy Spirit and giving testimony to the freedom of God (pp. 123-24).

It is important to note the way in which Ellul envisions the place of the Scriptures in ethics. This article emphasizes these two points: that biblical commands are not constraints, but must be understood within the overarching framework of the freedom of the gospel; and that these commands are not necessarily to be followed literally, but yet are to be understood as having concrete content (pp. 124-25). These comments advocating a guiding function for the biblical prescriptions contradict Ellul's earlier absolute rejection of a moral stance (p. 121), for in recommending the Scriptures as aids for choosing what is profitable for the neighbor he seems to defend an occasionalistic consequentialism, an ethical method of making decisions for a particular situation on the basis of the outcome or effects to others. The problem illustrates the difficulty of holding together the dialectic of freedom and love that Ellul establishes, without falling into either a new law or libertinism.

Besides love, the other criterion for freedom, according to Paul (and Ellul), is the glory of God (pp. 125-28) — that our lives actually manifest God's freedom. Ellul usually pursues this theme from the negative side, in his frequent critiques of sacralization, of giving glory to false gods. The human aggrandizement that has fabricated a "Christianity" which has "voluntarily forsaken revelation and the Lord" and thereby "opted for a new bondage" is the main target of Ellul's denunciation in *The Subversion of Christianity* (1984/86). Both *A Critique of the New Commonplaces* (1966/68) and *The New Demons* (1973/75) are thorough criticisms of modern divinizations; *Money and Power* (1954, 1979/1984) challenges Christians to stop sacralizing Mammon in order to hear God's question to us concerning our money. Only occasionally in *The Ethics* and in *The Presence of the Kingdom* (1948/51) does Ellul use the positive phrase "the glory of God"; usually he chooses other descriptions.

Ellul's other emphases here — the warning not to return to bondage, especially that of morality and systems (pp. 128-29); the insistence that it is a question not of a "good use of freedom," but of its very existence (p. 129); the differentiation between "the free person (which we are not) and the freed person (which we will never cease to be)" (p. 130); and the concluding reminder that our freedom takes its value only in the measure that it is a sign of the freedom of God (p. 131) — are all elaborated in *The Ethics*. Throughout his career Ellul followed the apostle Paul in trying to awaken us to our slavery to the powers of the world and in urging us to watch so that we do not lose our freedom by separating it from the love and glory of God (p. 131).

CHAPTER 6

"The Contemporaneity of the Reformation"

SOURCES

Fourteen years before this article appeared, Ellul published a piece entitled "The Current Significance of the Reformation."[1] Although that article was written much earlier than the one included here, the latter was chosen instead because it was written after and in the midst of Ellul's involvement in ecumenical and national church organizations.

From 1947 to 1951 Ellul served in the commissions of the World Council of Churches, but he left that organization voluntarily. In the 1981 interviews recorded as *In Season, Out of Season,* he remarked, "if I sometimes react violently on the subject of the Ecumenical Council, it is because of the experience I had there that taught me that at the present time we can hope for very little real spiritual progress from the council and also that its sociopolitical studies and messages are pretty worthless."[2] In 1951 Ellul became a member of the National Council of the French Reformed Church. During this time he and his friend Jean Bosc (who preceded Ellul as editor of *Foi et Vie*) were especially con-

1. Jacques Ellul, "Signification actuelle de la Reforme," *Protestantisme français,* ed. Marc Boegner and André Siegfried (Paris: Plon, 1945), pp. 137-65.
2. Ellul, *In Season, Out of Season: An Introduction to the Thought of Jacques Ellul,* based on interviews with Madeleine Garrigou-Lagrange, trans. Lani K. Niles (San Francisco: Harper & Row, 1982), p. 67.

cerned about revising the curriculum of the seminaries and making lay people aware of their role as Christians in their society. Again Ellul became greatly disillusioned, because only the leaders were interested in his ideas. The people had no say, so the leaders took over, and as a result their powers increased in a legalistic and bureaucratic way. (This was what Ellul had also experienced politically after World War II.) Though Ellul left the council in 1970 and in general lost interest in denominational structures, he had started a church in his home in Pessac in 1953 and continued to preach and lead Bible studies there throughout most of the rest of his life.

Ellul's repetitive vocabulary is retained particularly for the following article since he frequently uses recurrent words to highlight comparisons. The major underlying opposition he stresses is that between the paradigmatic biblical fidelity of the Protestants and the lack of it on the part of the (only rarely named) Roman Catholic Church.

This article presents Ellul's understanding of how the principal ideas of the Protestant Reformation worked themselves out in history, which is, of course, influenced by the French Protestant perspectives of his own time. We won't find in this essay any recognition of the nitty-gritty conflicts, the mistakes and confusions, Luther's horrible treatises against the peasants or the Jews — elements of history that we who follow the Reformers confess, repent of, and try to avoid in the present. By the same token, we will find hardly any of the key doctrines that Luther or Calvin rediscovered and that are still vitally important for our faith lives. What Ellul gives us instead is a challenge to be the Church as he envisions it should be.

The Contemporaneity of the Reformation

Jacques Ellul

If the Reformation retains a contemporary significance for our own society, it is certainly not owing to a formal, external fidelity to the principles that inspired it. It would negate the Reformation itself to wish to maintain in the form in which they were then fixed both the understanding of Scripture and the formulation of that dogma, as well as the ecclesiastical institution or its place in society. We cannot at all consider the teachers of the Reformation as infallible interpreters of the will of God, frozen in immortality. That would be to reject exactly the most significant element of their teaching, the challenging of our entire religious and ecclesiastical achievements by the Word of God itself, and, in what concerns the [Christian] presence in the world, [it would be to fail to take account of] the fact that [the Reformers] were attentive exactly to the concrete reality of this world, directly involved in its tendencies and temptations; and our society is no longer theirs [so that we should not copy their solutions]. What assuredly remains characteristic [and therefore applicable in our situation] is first of all this very presence. Political events, in France, in England, in the ["Holy Roman"] Empire, found [the Reformers] involved in all the quarrels [of the Reformation century], but even more in all the quests for a new form of the exercise of power. And the intellectual movement, the social demands were at each instant inspired or combatted by this effort. The Reformers teach us in any case that the Church cannot be separated from the world and folded back upon itself, no more than [it can be] manager and regent toward a world that will be subject to it.

"Actualite de la Réforme," *Foi et Vie* 58, 2 (March/April 1959): 39-64.

But the double difficulty of comprehending their action on society belongs first to the fact that this action is never for them anything other than the consequence of their fidelity to the Revelation, to the Word of their Lord. If they exercised this or that influence, it is not by virtue of their political ideas, of their metaphysical doctrines, of their social ideology, nor moreover according to their societal loyalties, to their class interests, to their economic location within a certain sociologically determined group. They were men of the Word, and consciously, voluntarily, they attempted to act on society according to this sole loyalty, to this voluntary determination. Thus we need to try to understand how this or that political decision, or, more generally, this attitude with regard to the civilization of their time, was derived from this understanding. And we cannot limit ourselves to reproducing that, for two elements of the relationship have changed. On the one hand, their interpretation of Scripture does not necessarily impose itself on us as is and by way of authority; on the other hand, all the elements of the world have been modified. It is no longer possible for us to speak of the state as Calvin spoke of it, when every prince claimed to be Christian. It is no longer possible to speak of scientific or technical work, as Erasmus spoke of it, when every investigator and savant acknowledged himself first a creature of the Sovereign Lord. Other perspectives have opened up before us.

The second element of difficulty proceeds from the unconscious and involuntary character of the greatest part of the consequences of their work. There was a whole set of more or less indirect effects of the Reformation that were not willed, expressly foreseen, delimited, stated. These are not perhaps the least important. They seem to have penetrated much more deeply into the structure of the society, to have acted much more slowly and more directly in what might almost be called the collective unconscious.

There are some results there, perhaps unforeseen, contained nevertheless in the stating of such theological truth, of a similar conscious will to obey. And what stemmed from it was diverse; some [results] seem to us a remarkable achievement, which there should be no question of abandoning in our society: secularization of the State, desacralization of the World, new awareness of the person ... Other [results] seem like wormy fruits from the same root: the bourgeois spirit, capitalism, setting loose the will to power . . . Thus it is necessary for us to know that, in testing in our turn obedience and fidelity to the Revealed Word, a whole set of consequences will escape us,[1] which we cannot foresee, and that there will also be, whatever might be our desire and our prayer, wormy fruits borne of the very fact that we belong to this world and that we cannot pretend to escape its contaminations if we are present to it. But what matters, the only thing, is the most exact obedience within the very conditions of this presence. The only two paths that are forbidden us are [first] the concern for a fidelity so pure, a theology so transcendent that it leads to accepting all human conduct, defined by sociological forces, [and second,] the opposite, the search for a certain interpretation of the Bible, for a certain theology, in order to legitimize a [certain] social doctrine, the taking of a political position, a sentimental impulse — and both of these are, in the end, the same betrayal.

*　　　*　　　*

Assuredly one of the most important consequences of the Reformation with regard to the world was the desacralization of diverse forms. The Reformers reminded [people] vigorously that God is in heaven and human beings are on earth; that the world is the locus of the Prince of this world; that human beings are by nature and definitively sinners and without any possibility of doing the good;[2] the world is the world. It is in no way inhabited by sacred powers; nothing in the world exceeds the greatness of humankind; there is no mystery in the world; there are no more natural barriers than meaning itself.[3]

1. It is not clear if Ellul means that these consequences will get out of our control or that they will escape our attention or perception.
2. Though Ellul doesn't specifically mention it, his sparring partner here is Reformation-age Catholicism, as understood by French Protestants in his era. Ellul's theological perception is that sixteenth-century Catholicism's confidence in "nature" and "reason" connotes an inadequate sense of fallenness.
3. We can see in these early comments from Ellul the disenchantment in the natural world that later led to such explicating notions as the "secular city" of Harvey Cox. The basic idea is that because the world has no eerie edges, no mysterious sacred powers, science can understand it without remainder. Nature has no "meaning in itself"; the observer gives it its meaning.

The presence of the sacred at the interior of this world indeed intrinsically guarantees a meaning to events and to history: people know on their own what they are doing and where they are going; this is said to them, guaranteed by the presence of the sacred within history, within things, within nature. That same sacred, moreover, sets limits to human action: there are taboos; there are things one can [do] and things one cannot. There is what is licit and what is illicit: not because of a human edict, because of some express prohibition, but by the very nature of things, by the natural order, by a truth infused in the world. And from one [the licit] as from the other [the illicit] a scale of values stretches out; in a way that cannot be refused, the sacred furnishes people with the discernment of good and of evil, the desirable and the sublime, in the face of which there is not any hesitation or critique. And patiently the medieval scholasticism, assuming a world inhabited by the sacred, had sewn [together] stitch by stitch a Christian theology concerning the social world, had elaborated a sacred [system] derived from Christianity, encompassing, modulating the sacred from nature. Slowly the church had sacralized what could claim some autonomy — the power of the state, like the pagan rites of the guilds or of chivalry. That meant, then, adopting the laws of Christian morality as a sacred prohibition for all of society and the perspective of the [last] Judgment as the sacralization of meaning. That meant finding in everything the point of connection between nature and grace, between the reality of the world and the truth of God, between the humanly possible and the demand of the Spirit. And consequently one establishes, as an expression of this sacrality, a whole intermediary world, that of saints and of witches, that (which is the same) of natural law and of reason as *imago Dei*, that of merit and of implicit faith, that of the temporal power of the church reunited with the sacralization of the state. The entire problem was to know where and how, in this intermediate world, the sacredness of God was infused into the sacredness of the world.

And here the Reformers brutally interfere with this subtle, delicate construction; here they "reject in one stroke a thousand years of nearly univocal theology" and tear the easily woven fabric. There is no sacrality in the world; neither the state nor even the church is sacred any more. Things are what they are: there aren't any spirits

140

in them at all; matter is matter, even that of human beings. There is nothing venerable in nature — history has no significance in itself; nothing is in itself, by itself prohibited; people left to themselves are blind, incapable of any good, and destined to death. If history makes sense, it is by the attribution of an extrinsic meaning, coming from God. If human beings do the good, it is by the extrinsic action of God, who acts upon them by grace, and no possible continuity exists between nature and grace. . . . The world desacralized then becomes again fully the world. Not a world without law, but a world that does not have the same laws as the church, a world that cannot be Christianized from the outside, with reference to which the hypocrisy of acting as if it were Christian cannot work, as if the sacrality that it wants and secretes were anything but idolatry, illusion, falsehood, and rejection of God.

This desacralization has entailed innumerable consequences. From then on it was no longer possible to live in illusion. We were awakened brutally into a world unleashed — human beings have laid hands on everything because nothing was sacred to them any more. Then the great adventure of technology began. Everything was permitted henceforth in this world. One no longer had to fear the vengeance of the spirits that had fled things.[4] By the same blow the great questioning began. Everything could be subjected to doubt, everything could be up for grabs: the power of the state, like that of parents, like social hierarchy; all this was merely natural and therefore subject to the critique of reason — thus natural human beings ought to act, taking on themselves their [natural] condition in a world and a society that had been given back into their hands. Consequently the situation was honest and clear. The church did not have to exert power over this world and these people, nor to impose laws on them. All that it could do was to proclaim the Word of God over this world and these people, to testify by its works, and the life of Christians, and their words, to the work accomplished by God in this world and on behalf of these human beings.

Thus [what was] in the first place established was no longer a conciliation, a synthesis between the Revelation and the natural order, but an entirely new situation, a tension between two forces,

4. I.e., since people no longer believed that spirits inhabited things.

of radically different quality, whose origin and end are equally opposed. This stood out very profoundly on the level of the state. Instead of claiming a subordination of the Christian state to the church, a channeling [of power, authority] within the hierarchy of these two powers, the Reformation inaugurates a liberation of the state with regard to the church — the state is no longer Christian. It is itself. It has a certain function, moreover, inscribed in the plan of God. And the church can only address it to establish a dialogue in which it announces to this state the will of the Wholly Other, the word that must, by itself alone and without any system of exterior, juridical, political constraint, induce this state into just politics and into a voluntary acceptance of the service of God. The letters of Calvin to the king of England are very significant in this respect.[5]

But this consideration of the duality of the church and the world led to a second consequence: beginning from the moment when there was no more sacrality included in the world, the decision about the conduct of life depends on the person. Human beings are placed before the Word of God; they are affected, and they must personally form an opinion. They are responsible for their response. They are no longer included in an order that carries everyone naturally, spontaneously toward Christian behavior even if the person scarcely has conviction. The upheaval brought about by the Reformation is that one cannot be Christian by being aware, by obeying nature, by following a law of inertia; faith presupposes consciousness, voluntary appropriation, and the development of a certain culture. To become Christian is an act against nature, and this Christian is then called, in this society, to affirm God's demands, for, when I was saying above that the church is situated in this state of tension in relation to the world, that had to do less with eccle-

5. Calvin wrote to Edward VI on July 4, 1552, and sent him four sermons, including one that urged believers to prize the privilege of being in the Church of God and another that exhorted the faithful to flee from idolatry. In his letter he urged the king to "submit [him]self with all humility and reverence beneath the spiritual sceptre of [the great King's] Gospel." John Calvin, *Letters, Compiled from the Original Manuscripts and Edited with Historical Notes*, 4 vols., ed. Jules Bonnet, trans. M. R. Gilchrist and David Constable (1858; repr. New York: Burt Franklin, 1973), vol. 2, pp. 354-55.

siastical authorities (which the Reformation stripped of their pres-
tige and their exclusivity) than with the faithful themselves, where
they each find themselves. Of course, there can scarcely be hope
that all will accept this Word of God and become Christians. The
majority of people, probably, will belong to the secular world (although that did not seem evident to the Reformers, who lived in a
strongly Christianized society, which could delude them). But at
least let these [secular] people know what they are doing; let them
be placed before their responsibilities; let all unclarity be dissipated.
Let the non-Christians behave as non-Christians, and let their motives be unveiled (that corresponds to the famous reputation of
Protestants for honesty and rigor!). The individual is thus sum-
moned to becoming aware, and this was without doubt the second
great work of the Reformation! Becoming aware of oneself, of one's
motivations, of one's autonomy and of one's responsibility. Becoming aware of the world in which one is situated, of its contestations
and of its conflicts. Becoming aware of the Word of God, of its
personal truth and of its objectivity: thus at every level the individual is aroused. But while that leads the Christian to more
authenticity in the faith, it leads those who refuse to self-affirmation,
to the exaltation of the individual, to the pride of those who claim
to define their destiny on their own. By the same blow this opens
up a contestation [that is] at the same time religious, political, intellectual, economic. Now individuals no longer see any limit to
their possibilities, to their enterprises. They can carry their con-
structive powers everywhere. Everything depends on their own
decision. No longer are there rules in themselves; no longer is there
an order imposing itself upon them even if they reject the will of
God. The dilemma is rigid — *either* they recognize this will, and
then they enter into obedience, into an order, into the work of God,
in which they participate, not only spiritually, but also in the realm
of the political, of labor, of intelligence, *or else* they reject the
revelation, and then they find themselves without brakes, without
any other authority than themselves, for from this moment the state,
justice, morality, etc., which don't have any value in themselves, are
hence their own work. They are the master of all that; thus the
decision taken by the individual takes on an extraordinary weight.
The person is appealed to in everything; one can no longer avoid

trying to be oneself. Without doubt the Reformers did not see clearly that their theology, conformed to Scripture, would lead to this point. Luther sometimes had misgivings. But this consequence was truly included [in the implications of the Reformation message]. And human beings, in the course of their history, have followed through with it.

*   *   *

Now, while the Reformation was being born, a new world was being born at the same time. [There was] transformation on every level of society: political with the formation of nations, economic with the triumph of the bourgeois economy over the feudal economy, intellectual with the Renaissance. What seems very remarkable to me is the fact that the Reformation was neither a defender of the Christian past nor a support without reservation for this new society. We easily accept the first point, call attention to everything that the Reformation rejected of the medieval heritage, insist on its progressive character; however, the situation was much more complex, and in their fidelity to the Revelation the Reformers were unceasingly led to pronounce a Yes, but also a No, in the face of the new truth and of the human initiatives, as they pronounced a No but also a Yes with respect to the traditional society nearing disappearance. Sometimes voluntarily, sometimes involuntarily, they attempted to preserve a large part of the tradition, of the heritage. Likewise, they sifted through the sieve of a dense critique every innovation of the sixteenth century. It is evidently very difficult to demonstrate that in a few pages. All that one could say about it is inevitably superficial. It was already hazardous, in the effervescence of the sixteenth century, to want to draw the boundaries between what is traditional and what is novelty. There is never a tradition that does not at this moment try to put on a new face. Nothing is created that does not have roots immersed in the Middle Ages in general. Now, concerning this difficult division, it can seem impossible to attempt to graft together the division that the Reformers themselves have accomplished, reconciling their support for, and developing their critique toward, this or that intellectual or social movement. And yet, if we don't refine

144

to the extreme (which effectively removes all possibility of reflection), we can succeed in tracing a few main lines [that are] not too inexact.

Without any doubt, the Reformers rejected two methods of the old world, the scholasticism and the pedagogy. They equally challenged economic regulation. They condemned the exploitation of the poor by the rich and the oppression of the weak by the powerful. They attempted to destroy the pretension of the church to regulate civil society (without succeeding . . . Calvin at Geneva!). But above all they challenged the total integration of the individual into the social group. What they rejected was "Totality," the conception of a global society, the fact that the group was considered as a unity. Society was counted by households, by lordships, by towns. Then in the sixteenth century [the social units became] the countries, the states, the universities; people did not exist at all as themselves, but existed only by their group. The group was not made of individuals; the latter were only fragments of this primary unity. That is what the Reformers rejected, whether it be the family, the corporation, the nation . . . Yet inversely, they claimed to conserve from that traditional society the morality (the Reformers' ethic differs very little from the medieval ethic); the hierarchical structure of the society; the value of authority in everything — in the family, in the state, in the church; the monarchic form of power; respect for the creation and human nature in all its dimensions. Let us not claim that these [elements of ethical conservatism] were aberrant residues and that the Reformers lacked courage in not advocating liberalism or democracy; they knew these ideas quite well, as much as the proposed liquidation of traditional morality, and if they rejected them, it was perfectly with full knowledge of the facts, and because they estimated that the elements retained from medieval society were a more accurate expression of Christian thought. This [cultural conservatism] was not at all laziness or incoherence, but an effort of discernment and fidelity. Of course, sometimes, some attachment remains that can appear astonishing. Calvin often retains a scholastic style of thought and cites some authors, like Peter Lombard, who seem to us extraordinarily contrary to the Reformation. But that very [thought] should lead us to reflect on our own understanding of the Reformation and on its concern to conserve from the old

145

order as much as possible. We know well that it was not light-heartedly that Luther broke up the *continuity* not only of the church, but also of the society in which he found himself. He did not do that in the thought that it was all worthless, but with respect for all that exists which people, including himself, should not oppose — neither lightly, nor by ignorance (which is quite often the case), nor by concern to be in the vanguard of progress, but [only] because one cannot do otherwise out of fidelity to the Lord.

By the inclination to be in the vanguard of progress . . . , certainly the Reformers never had this inclination, so frequent in our Protestant churches today. Toward new movements they had the same spirit of discernment as toward the old society. Without any doubt, they contributed to the breakup of the *corpus Christianum* and to the formation of national unities. That corresponded exactly to the tendency to desacralize the world, to a new vision of human collectivities, to the legitimation of non-Christian political forms. By the same token, they advanced along the dangerous path of national autonomy; they went with the stream of the states and of demography, and they justified the fact. It is at least legitimate to observe sometimes that this fact corresponds to a certain conception of the truth, although we remain concerned not to conform our vision of revelation to facts that exist, quite simply because that would be to recognize an authority ultimately superior to the Revelation.[6] It does not seem that the Reformers yielded to that [temptation]. Likewise, in the new world they affirmed the dignity of labor and its liberty. In the face of the medieval conception insisting especially on the characteristic of penalty, on the necessity of restricting labor, and on its lack of meaning, the Reformers marched into the new age with this conviction that those who labor are responding to a vocation which is addressed to them by God, and that also in laboring they participate in the divine work; that the earth and all it contains were given to human beings to show this hidden wealth to advantage, to realize its potential. Consequently, they favored the development of "mechanical skills" and asserted both that all technical enterprise was legitimate

6. In other words, Ellul disapproves of theologians supporting the formation of modern nationalism, but he grants that the Reformers who bought into nationalism were acting according to their best understanding of the truth at that time.

and, at the same time, that the manual laborer had dignity before God, because he was obeying the will of God and because it was useful to all. Lastly, it is evident that the Reformers also advanced in the direction of the new society by their participation in the Renaissance. The book, the reading, the search for the authenticity of the text, the knowledge of ancient authors outside of all prejudice, of all dogmatic limit — how could the men of the book, the men of the Return to the origins, not have supported to the utmost all this intellectual effort? And similarly with the will to know facts in their exactitude, to observe what exists in its reality (which leads at the same time to rejecting fables and sorceries, to analyzing without preconceptions, and to traveling in order to learn what lies beyond our horizon), all that would encounter the full agreement of the Reformers, considering that the world is a creation of God and that we have to know this creation well in order to discern in it the wisdom and the love of the Creator, which cannot be done amid illusion and lies. But this is far from meaning that the Reformers gave support without limit, approbation without reserve to the blossoming of the Renaissance. We know to what degree Erasmus and Luther were opposed on the intellectual level. That is representative of everything else: human beings glorious in their youthful, freshly acquired intelligence proclaim "myself, nothing but myself" and affirm their autonomy, their metaphysical freedom as well as their civil liberty — to which Luther responds with the most firm, the most rigorous No. This entire Renaissance enterprise is by him consigned to the demon if it leads human beings to that kind of grandeur, and the solitary pride of an ascetic Stylite does not look very different to the Reformers from the other solitary pride of the creative humanist incarnated by da Vinci; the man in revolt, the man who fails to recognize his Creator and his Savior, they discern him perfectly in the Renaissance man and reject that radically, both when it was the peasants' revolt and when it was the intellectual revolt of a Castellion,[7] for what they await is not, finally, a human order, but the Lord himself. And we find the same

7. Castellion was a radical reformer who protested against the execution of Servetus, an early Anabaptist, and against the religious wars between Protestants and Catholics. Some French Protestants see him as a precursor of Protestant liberalism.

firmness in a quite different aspect of the expansion of the Renaissance, in that of wealth, of luxury, of art for art's sake, of the easy life. If labor is legitimate, if human beings are called to accomplish all that their hand finds to do, it is neither to exploit creation nor for their own happiness; it is uniquely in order to obey a vocation and likewise to render glory to God by this means. It would not be a question of devoting human strength to improve one's standard of living, nor to develop one's comfort or ease (the moral discipline of the Reformed was strongly hostile to the easy life). Wealth and the accumulation of capital are all treated as severely by Calvin as by the theologians of the Middle Ages, and nowhere did the Reformers accept [the idea] that lending at interest could be unlimited and a legitimate source of wealth. They tolerated it only in certain cases. In the realm of art, they never made aesthetic value the kind of value that justified the work: to their eyes not everything is permitted as long as it is "art"! Beauty, too, is called to be a servant of the Lord, and when it is not it is demonic and cannot expect any sort of indulgence on the part of the Creator. If then the Reformers were able to say this No to the new world which was coming into being and in which they were participants, it is for the same reason that they could justify their Yes. They did not resist by traditionalism, by staying in line with the past, by lack of nerve, but only by fidelity to the Revelation. It is not necessary to hold either of the two judgments that, humanly, we are tempted to hold: that if they said Yes, it was in conformity to the progressivism of their epoch, and if they said No, it was out of traditionalism; or again, that in saying Yes they were faithful and [that they were] unfaithful in saying No. We can multiply our judgments, each according to our tastes and opinions. But the sole effort of the Reformers was to express their fidelity to the Word of God. It is not for us today to ask whether they succeeded.

*   *   *

But it is assuredly asked of us today to adopt the same attitude — namely, [to be] present to the modern world, to search for what is by [its] relationship to this world really faithful to the will of the Lord, [that] will [which is] both permanent, eternal, objective, identical with itself, and also present, innovative, subjective, and

148

expressed *hic et nunc.* Such fidelity can absolutely not be expressed in a pure and simple rejection of the way the world is going, and no more [can it be expressed] in an adhesion to one or another of the proposed forms, neither to a "passé-ism" of conserving dead values, nor to a "progressivism" of exalting existing values. All that is of the order of fidelity to history, which is the same when it concerns fidelity to the past history of our great ancestors of whom we want to be worthy, or [when it concerns] fidelity to the direction of history, taught by Marx, and which charts our duty: they come back to the same thing. From the outset we must enunciate a rigorous and total No to such fidelity whatever might be the direction in which it is formulated. History is not the Lord, despite the quite numerous writings of contemporary Christians who would try to make us believe that! And there is no other fidelity to have than that toward the Revealed Word, even if it be contradictory to the course of history, even if it should engage us in repudiating the great examples of the past or in rejecting the necessary evolution toward socialism . . . Now, today in this milieu of the twentieth century, our situation is at once like that of the Reformers and unlike it. It is alike in that we live in a world of upheavals equivalent to those of the sixteenth century. One can say that there have been other such times, 1789 for example. Well, as paradoxical as this might seem, I'll dare to say no. As a matter of fact, there have been spectacular troubles in 1789 or 1914,[8] [but they have been only] on the façade; but in the sixteenth century the situation was different — what had to be changed was not a form of government, but the very pivot of the society itself: one passed from a theocentric society to an "anthropocentric" society. And that is expressed from the outset in the paintings, in the literature, and in the structures of the society. In this direction, the revolution of 1789 as well as the absolute state of Louis XIV or the age of the Enlightenment are only the consequences of this mutation at the center of the society — normal, foreseeable consequences, and only consequences, not at all innovation. This is, moreover, well known and repeated by a thousand authors. Now,

8. I.e., the years of the beginnings of the French Revolution and of World War I.

in our time, we are taking part in the same revolution: society is changing afresh from the center, the pivot; it is once again a Copernican revolution that is being produced. From the anthropocentric society, which lasted from the sixteenth to the twentieth century, we are moving to the technocentric society. The supreme value is technique, in relation to which are organized society, the state, both the concrete and the intellectual life; technique takes precedence. And the painting and the literature are equally witnesses to it. Mounier,[9] who was not suspected of exaggerating the technical phenomenon, nor of fearing it, said that since the prehistoric era human beings had not encountered a greater mutation than this entry into the technical era. Thus this change of the center of society places us today in the same situation as the Reformers. Today? Certainly! For it is only in the last twenty years that human beings are becoming conscious of this fact. In 1900 no one realized what was happening. And the first stutterings of human beings opposed to technique, besides representing technique only by the Machine, were poetic lamentations without depth.

But on the other hand, our situation is entirely different from that of the people of the Reformation. From two points of view. In the first place, we know now that on the political, economic, and social levels the enterprise of the Reformers ended in failure. By their liberation of the world and engaging in a tension with it (and I repeat that I believe they had good motive, from a biblical point of view), they unchained the monster, and the monster was too strong for them. They were not able, in the dialogue with the state, to prevent it from becoming totalitarian, authoritarian, nationalistic. They were not able, in the elaboration of a Christian ethic, to prevent Christians from forming a capitalistic economy and giving free rein to the power of money. They were not able, in the preaching of grace, to move people to recognize themselves as creatures,

---

9. Emmanuel Mounier was a leader in the personalist movement, and Ellul and his best friend Bernard Charbonneau helped him to begin its journal *Esprit*. In 1937 Ellul broke with the movement for theological reasons and because of differing perspectives on how to accomplish social transformation. In the following comments and in Ellul's complaint later (pp. 159-60) about the loss of the person, we can see why Ellul was drawn to Mounier's work in the first place.

and so people declared themselves the measure of all things, without master and without duty. It is assuredly the risk of every authentic Christian position adopted. It was the same risk during the first three centuries of the Church. And the reaction of prudence was to avoid the risk by erecting the enormous machinery of rules, of laws, of moralities, of organizations, which became the Roman [Catholic] Church. That was effective. But revealed truth died of it. That kind of prudence is not the way for us to be prudent. The Reformers knew the risk of faith. They placed society in the same situation of this risk. Truth was rekindled, but human sin rendered the fruits of it bitter. Well, now we know that; we are no longer in the situation of innocence that was possible in the sixteenth century. We know the danger. We are the children of that scorching. And we can no longer plunge ahead with the belief that things will turn out well because the truth will be proclaimed, that society will be happy because the Church will be just and faithful. We would more easily have the opposite conviction, and because of this fact we will be inclined not to involve ourselves in this adventure, to stay by ourselves, or again to reconnect Christianity to a social doctrine that itself would be a guarantee for society at the same time that our faithfulness to Jesus Christ would be a guarantee of truth. This doctrine could be socialism or liberalism; these attitudes are equally inadequate and lead to the same heresy as Constantinianism. Thus the experience and the failure of the Reformers lead us to look twice before doing anything, and we are then often led to do nothing.

Our situation is different from that of the sixteenth century from a second point of view: the sixteenth century was still a Christian century; the churches had a dominant position from a social, economic, or intellectual perspective; Christianity was a point of reference for everyone; it was practically the only global intellectual system, the only possible form of thought, and even agnostic tendencies were located within a Christian framework, as Lucien Febvre[10] has shown. Consequently, what happened in the church had great

10. Lucien Febvre (1878-1956) was a highly respected historian; one of his books was *Un destin Martin Luther.* He and Marc Bloch (1886-1944) were founders of a school of social history, along with its organ, the *Annales d'Histoire Sociale.*

151

importance. Everyone took ecclesiastical conflicts seriously. Everyone had an opinion with regard to the behavior of the monks or to the reformation of the church (not to dogma!). Everyone was touched by the same fact of the church's influence. Theological discussions, even when nothing was understood, seemed important and had actual repercussions on the society; and when schism or a reformation happened, the crowd participated in it, because it was the belief itself of these people that was modified and because it was the structure of an essential part of their life that changed. What the Reformers then could say or do theologically accordingly had actual repercussions on people's behavior.

But today! Christianity is a residue from the past; at best, people consider it as a system of beliefs and thought, a little old, having good credentials, and located on a complex map among thousands of philosophical, economic, and political systems, each having its own value, and a legitimate value. From a concrete point of view, the church, even the Roman [Catholic Church], no longer has great influence. When it intervenes politically or socially, it appears to non-Christians like a force seeking to be involved in what is not its business. They are happy to leave it its place, which is the spiritual [realm], but it should not leave its ghetto, except to put its little influence at the service of some order of the state. It is good that the Orthodox Church support the war of the Soviet state and its movement for peace. It is good that the Baptist or Presbyterian churches support the anti-communism of the American state. It is good that the German Protestant Church not support Hitler's revolution.[11] No farther than that. A church annexed by the dominant political-social current, that is what can be tolerated. In these conditions it is understandable that theological discussions don't have any importance for the people of the world and are contemplated with a commiserating smile: "These intellectuals, all the same!" We

11. This is an odd combination. Two of the examples Ellul cites are pro-state positions of mainstream churches, which often happen. The third example is a minority resistance idea that barely happened. Pastor Charles says that many French Protestants at the time this article was written held up the model (in an exaggerated way) of the German Confessing Church (of which Dietrich Bonhoeffer and Karl Barth are the most well-known members) as an example to show that Protestantism's theological principles could see through political ideologies.

all know that very well, and that is why we cannot take quite seriously the kind of reflection I am carrying on here. Even if we knew clearly what is necessary for us to be, what is necessary for us to do in order to be faithful to the Revelation, our decisions, our attitudes, our declarations would not have great value, neither toward the authorities nor to an economic point of view, nor toward the masses. This is thus totally different from the sixteenth century. We know this well, and that leads us to a certain discouragement: "What good is it to take so much trouble to think exactly; what good is it to seek the right attitude of fidelity, since it will not have any effect, since no one listens to us; then we cannot engage in conversation with anyone, and then in terms of efficacity we are reduced to nothing." I want to say very simply that the problem is not *first of all* of efficacity, but *first of all* of fidelity. What matters is obedience — and that we have to attempt no matter what [the prospects]. It is fitting to remember here the centuries of silence in the course of Israel's history: the great silence of God for perhaps two hundred years during the slavery in Egypt between the period of Joseph and that of Moses, and the great silence of God for nearly four hundred years between Esdras and the last prophets and the appearance of John the Baptist. During those centuries of absence, the question for Israel was how to maintain hope and fidelity, despite and against all reason. That is our question.

* * *

It seems to me that we are called in our turn to situate ourselves in relation to this new world, but also in relation to the old world that is passing away. Our situation is a nearly inextricable mingling of one and the other, and yet one can succeed in discerning what belongs to one and the other, what is waning and what is dawning, and we cannot without the other bury what is disappearing any more than we can welcome automatically what is coming. A sorting out remains to be done, even if it be useless, tentative, the most vain; what matters is if it is in line with the truth. As to the old world, perhaps we will easily agree not to regret some elements that are disappearing. Traditional capitalism, with the private seizure of the powers of production, with the exploitation of one person by

153

another, with the building of an entire society around money, and, eventually, with the escalation of useless production and incoherent distribution — all of that cannot leave us with regrets; we cannot be attached to this form in which injustice and inhumanity have surpassed in volume and in density everything that existed before in leading astray what could have been a source of good for all. Likewise for colonialism, linked to capitalism, the so-called legitimate conquest of "savage countries," the unrestrained exploitation of natural resources, the contempt for peoples [who are] inferior because [they have been] conquered — [all of this] under the semblance of civilization, of raising living standards, and of introducing Christianity. The term *semblance* introduces us to one of the characteristics undoubtedly most important in this society: its hypocrisy. Imperialistic colonization that justifies itself by idealistic motivations (and that it represents only in appearance), like capitalism justifying itself by virtue of individual and economic freedom or by virtue of the human vocation to labor, etc. Hypocrisy finds its highest expression in the affirmation of freedom while subjecting human beings to the worst enslavement. Now, let us be very attentive, for we live fully in the midst of this hypocrisy characteristic of this waning world — it is in the name of the Spirit that the most virulent technologists (Sauvy,[12] Fourastié,[13] etc.) developed technique; it is in the name of freedom that the individual is regulated, planned, organized, materially and psychologically conditioned — and hypocrisy was proper to the Hitlerian and Stalinist regimes, as it is *in the same way* to the present Soviet regime. We are probably [with those regimes] in the presence of the tragic legacy from the old world to the new. There would be many other things of the past world that we could bury without regret: the disincarnate individualism of the nineteenth century, formal democracy, idealistic scientism, etc., but we cannot dwell on them. The problem of the lethal legacy from the old world to the new seems to me more serious. I just cited collective hypocrisy; the other legacy to remem-

12. Alfred Sauvy wrote a *General Theory of Population* in 1956; the English translation was published in 1970.

13. Both Sauvy and Fourastié were members of Jean Monnet's planning team. Jean Monnet was the principal founder of the European Common Market.

ber is Nationalism. This form of sociopolitical structure, which becomes religious by virtue of the people's worship of their nation, would seem quite linked to [that of] Western society of the nineteenth century, which it led to its ruin amid disasters and blood. And notice that the Abomination is spilling out its power in the entire world — the Arabs become nationalists — the Africans and Asians become nationalists — the communists are nationalists, they whose doctrine contains still the leaven of an anti-nationalism! Now these diverse nationalisms present exactly the same characteristics as those of Western Europe, despite certain superficial analyses that might want to oppose them. It seems certain that the Church must struggle in every country against all of the aspects of these two vices of the old world, sociopolitical hypocrisy and nationalism, and must strive to profit from the change of social structures in order to move them along the path toward their disappearance.

On the other hand, we should try to save from our time certain acquisitions that are also threatened and that despite their weakness and their humility are authentic and good. As Christians and as Reformed Christians, we must be firmly attached to democracy. Not that it is a Christian regime, nor that it is ideal, nor that it presents more virtues than another [form of] government! But precisely in its weakness, in its possibility for disorder, in its uncertainties, in its possible inefficacity, it remains the most humane of regimes, the most capable of respect for human beings, the most open and, now, the most humble. It is not good in itself, but it no longer has the pretension of pride and does not believe itself to be Truth and Justice. God preserve us from any regime that claims itself the Truth, the Justice, and the Good! Democracy is relative, it knows itself as relative, and that is what makes us support it seriously. It alone offers a broad panoply of revealed tendencies; it alone allows the possibility for human beings from the outset not to be smothered. And it is for the same reason that we should defend laicity[14] in the face of states that claim to incarnate the truth and to discern the absolute; it is we Christians (because truth has been revealed) who must, in civil society, sustain the absence of a human and governmental truth, or, to take the

14. I.e., "separation of church and state."

positive aspect, must sustain laicity. We must take quite seriously everything that is contained in this term, which I enumerate in four propositions: [1] no power in the world can express truth in itself, because human beings never recognize anything but truths, fragments, and never absolutes, and in every human opinion there are parcels of these human truths; [2] all opinions must consequently be able to be expressed freely in society; we absolutely cannot ask the state to assume in some fashion what might be Christian truth: the Church alone has to take on this mission without outward aid; [3] the state, because [it is] laicized, never has the right to become absolute, for it can never itself take part in the debate about the truth, and therefore can never constrain its subjects absolutely; [and 4] a laicized state is necessarily a limited state, a moderate state.

Finally, among the acquisitions of the world that is waning, I would also retain Reason; a strange thing that today Christians should be the defenders of reason! But this is well within the Reformed tradition, being opposed to magic, to mystery, to popular credulity, and reclaiming the exercise of right reason in appropriating even the Revelation. Now, in the time that is coming, we behold an unleashing of delirium, a negation of reason; whether in the West it is a matter of a "bandwagon" collective mentality, of obedience to sociological currents, of the furious appeal to the dark forces of the unconscious, of propaganda, or in communist society of the development of schemas, stereotypes, prejudices, irrational beliefs (on which rest all of communism), everywhere it is a negation of the simple and firm, modest, but rigorous use of reason. Amid this unleashing of passions, we must call people back to reason, and the failure of the nineteenth century shows us that this is not easy;[15] now, what renders the matter much more difficult is that the words have lost their meaning! I have been saying "Democracy," "Laicity," "Reason"! But who could be against that! Everyone is in favor of democracy, laicity, reason: Hitler like Stalin, Khrushchev like [John Foster] Dulles, Debré

15. Pastor Charles suggests that this refers to the nineteenth century as having spawned the ideologies — Marxism, fascism, progress, etc. — that led to the disasters of the twentieth.

like Mollet![16] The words no longer have meaning. And here perhaps do we, Christians of the Reformation, have a quite singular vocation! Let us not forget that we are the people of the Word, that for us humble human speech is invested with a unique weight, for it is through it that the Revelation has made itself heard. Speech has received such fundamental dignity that the Son himself is called the Word! We cannot accept that language is simple convention. We cannot accept the collapse of language, nor that words no longer have meaning and that one can say anything whatever in any way whatever. It is on the level of speech that truth and falsehood are played out. And, for this reason, we ought to be very rigorous in the use of words. In dialogue with people, it will be necessary for us always to testify to the seriousness of the word, even the simply human [word]; it will be necessary for us unceasingly to remind people of the value of the words they employ, the commitment that they make when they use what has become for them no more than a handy formula. It will be necessary for us to be courageous enough to denounce [e.g., as follows] the fundamental lie of the one for whom a word is no more than a sound:

> you are allowed obviously to make a regime of adhesion,[17] a regime of plebiscites [with votes] of 99 percent, a regime where sincerity does not have the right to speak, where divergence of opinion is a crime, so the people must only receive and approve; but then don't call it democracy; there is the lie. You are allowed to have an exclusive doctrine, to have a state that claims to hold the truth and to explain to everyone and in every way, but then don't talk about laicity; there is the lie.

*   *   *

16. The latter two were opposing party leaders in France at the time Ellul wrote this piece. Michel Debré was a Gaullist, the Prime Minister (1959-62) who inaugurated the Fifth Republic. Guy Mollet was general secretary of the presocialist party and a previous Prime Minister (1956-57).

17. This is a technical term for a government that claims to be democratic since people vote on (that is, rubber stamp) what is proposed to them — i.e., they adhere without criticism.

This rigor concerning the value of words, this demand that our interlocutors know what they are saying, this ever-renewed affirmation that public persons (politicians, authors, economists, etc.) don't have the right to use words as formulae, this is what we must hold up against the great pretensions of the coming world. Everywhere it is shouted that this world must be one of justice, one of happiness for all (thanks to technique), one of reality correctly apprehended . . . I believe that the Reformed Christian cannot reject these . . . "values": Justice, of course — Happiness, perhaps — Realism, assuredly — but what do we mean! Let us be serious also in the use of these words. Let us not pretend that there can be two different justices according to classes or situations. Let us not pretend that justice is always what the government does, or the party, or the court. Let us not imply that this justice will be achieved through a maximum of injustice. Let us not say that you cannot make an omelet without breaking eggs;[18] let us do it, but let us stop calling it justice. At that moment [when we stop calling it justice] things will be in place and we shall know that the world which is coming, constructed by people who, [whether] on the right or the left, justify themselves thus, will not be and cannot be a world of justice, for whence would they, who so easily accept injustice toward their neighbor, have the slightest sense of what justice can be? We must be more demanding and more rigorous on the subject of the values that the world which is taking shape before our eyes claims to foster, on which it claims to be based — more demanding and more rigorous than the people who are in the process of constructing this world!

> You speak thus, so be it; but then we Christians, because after all we have some small idea of what justice is, and happiness, and reality, we demand that you be serious. It is not we who have whispered those words to you; you chose them yourselves. And imagine, those words concern us because they belong to the Revelation of God. And they are words that burn when one lies with them. These are words that explode when one wants to jam them

18. That is, breaking the eggs of maximum injustice in order to make the omelet of justice.

into the foundation of an edifice that is their contradiction. Just as the words *freedom* and *love* explode, from which the old world is in the process of dying.

The world that is being constructed claims to be realistic, but what seems most striking, to the contrary, is its unreality. On the one hand, people multiply political and economic doctrines, for example, and they claim to apply these doctrines and to inform society about these doctrines: this resurgence of idealism today is very striking and worrisome (whether the doctrine be about nationalisms, about planning, about federation, about communism, or about the American Way of Life!). On the other hand, everywhere an admirable optimism concerning human beings overflows. Human beings capable of taking in hand the meaning of techniques; human beings capable of using well, and for the good, the immense powers they possess — the state, providence suited to order all the problems, the planning that saves liberty — communist human beings who will have no more personal problems, human beings perfectly adapted to the technological society who have thereby become free people . . . All these formulae, encountered on every street corner in every country, seem to me prodigiously unrealistic. People refuse to look systematically straight at the reality of human beings, of the state, and of technique. And yet they claim to be building a realistic world. The Revelation also tells a certain number of things concerning these human beings and concerning this state. Our modest contribution to the world that is coming could be to remind it of these things, so that it can seriously base the values that it chooses for itself. And that would then be the Yes that we can seriously say to the society that is taking form. But at the same time, not less seriously, but with more passion and aggressivity, we must [also] say No. No to a world that wants to be total. No to a world that wants to be sacred. Here we find again the same debate as in the sixteenth century. For the world that is being organized before our eyes tends to reproduce the characteristics of the primitive world — and this [also] characterized the medieval world — the Totality and the Sacred. We find ourselves before a society that wants to be integrated, where there is no longer any distinction between the individual and the group, where the person/society

159

dilemma is resolved by identification: the person is realized only by means of and by way of society. This presupposes the formation of persons with a view to their own realization. The success of [Father] Teilhard is exactly the measure of this adhesion of the modern intellectual to this totality: the fusion of the individual conscience in the larger whole — the basic reality is the society, is the group; individuals no longer have existence in themselves; their sole vocation is to belong to a group and to express it; their sole virtue is to be useful to the group; their sole happiness is to be perfectly adapted to the group. It is the very formula of the prehistoric clan. We must be on guard against this totality that is being constituted before our eyes, as well in the U.S.S.R. as in the U.S.A., which is the very negation of all that human evolution has meant for the last 4,000 years: this difficult accession to individual consciousness, this difficult advance toward personal responsibility for one's destiny. I believe that the Reformers were certainly not mistaken when they proclaimed that no Christian faith is possible without that. And I believe, reciprocally, that Fr. Teilhard has formulated exactly an anti-Christianity (which, moreover, is not surprising: the incarnation of Jesus Christ has evaporated in his theory). I know, of course, all the arguments of our intellectuals to demonstrate that human beings are perfectly free, perfectly responsible in that world. Certainly I would not have the pretension to critique in two lines so many reassuring, and positive, and optimistic authorities. It seems to me that concrete reality all by itself has taken charge of critiquing them. The worry is that by the time one perceives that this critique with its object was correct, it will be too late, and the world will [already] be what it will be, and we shall no longer be able to do anything about it. At the same time that it becomes total, this world again becomes sacral. Religious objects proliferate around us. Everything asks us for adoration. Everything takes for human beings a value so eminent that one can no longer question anything. The Nation is an absolute value. Technique is the absolute Good. The State demands that we love and adore it. Productivity is the Great Way to Salvation. Independence is an unchallengeable truth, and little by little the American Way of Life and communism demand not some [degree of] reasonable evaluation, but rather the vocation, body and soul, without reserve, without limit. And this

160

entire beautiful reunified world requires from human beings all the sacrifices that only a God can demand: all their time, all their money, all their labor, all their love, and, of course, the sacrifice of their life, which is still the least, for previously it had demanded of them the sacrifice of their honor, of their dignity, of their conscience, and of their liberty. The first Christians who refused to sacrifice animals to false gods, the Reformers who refused to participate in the Mass or to light candles in front of statues were obviously people of little intelligence who had not understood everything that one owes to society and to collective Beliefs. They manifested a narrowness of spirit, a quite absurd intransigence. We now have a breadth of view, an allegiance toward reality, an intellectual suppleness that renders us apt to participate in the great collective sacrifice. We have especially remembered that it is necessary to render to Caesar what is his; and, indeed, when Caesar shows us that everything is his . . . , we still retain our small conscience. And here seems to me the point of an authentic commitment, that of a radical No to the sacralization of the world that is forming, to the subtle idols that always present themselves with evidence of the truth — the same evidence which was that of the Fruit, *beautiful* to see, *pleasant* to eat, *useful* for understanding: the three characteristics of our idols! And in so doing we only continue the will to fidelity to which the Reformers bore witness, fidelity to the Only One who is no idol.

TRAJECTORIES

Ellul rightly recognized that the Reformers' gift to us was not that they were infallible interpreters of the will of God, but he certainly idealizes them in this article when he claims instead that all they did was a consequence of their fidelity to the Revelation, to the Word of their Lord (p. 138). Though he definitely was not trying in his theological works to encourage contemporary Christians to reproduce the Reformers' political decisions, though he acknowledged throughout his career that their interpretations of the Scriptures are not necessarily authoritative for us (p. 138), he did consistently urge his fellow believers to try in our turn to be obedient and faithful to the Word revealed, without letting our task be defined by sociological forces or, on the other hand, without legitimizing a certain social doctrine by means of a slanted biblical interpretation (p. 139). This is the main point especially of his early book *The Presence of the Kingdom* (1948/51), which depicted the kingdom in terms of the Christian life standing always as a source of tension with the world's methods of doing things.

Ellul contends that one of the most important results of the Reformation for the world was the desacralizing of diverse forms of the Powers (pp. 139-42). This was always a key challenge in his later ethical works. *The Ethics of Freedom* (1973, 1975/1976) also recounts the desacralization of the Reformers and calls for similar despoiling of the present powers of the modern state, social utility, money, and the technological society. *The Humiliation of the Word* (1981/85) especially focuses on the powers of money, politics, and technique as it displays how language becomes their tool.

Ellul's emphasis on consciousness raising as the second great work of the Reformation of course identifies the great motivation for his own career. His two tracks of writing issued the same double call for awareness — that Christians should enter into obedience to God's will and participate in God's work not only spiritually but also in the domains of politics, vocation, and intelligence (p. 143) and that those who refuse the revelation will find themselves without a brake, without any other authority besides themselves (p. 143).

When Ellul insists that the Reformers themselves, in the midst of their times' transformations in all areas of society, were always guided by their efforts to be faithful to the Lord, he uses this overstatement as

162

a basis to criticize his contemporaries who were seeking to be progressive (pp. 144-46). Much the same critique is developed in *False Presence of the Kingdom* (1963/72), which both describes Ellul's perceptions of the factual situation of the Reformed Church of France (with its political involvements) and also attempts to impart a challenge similar to this article's call to be like the Reformers, who were as critically discerning toward new movements as they were toward the old (p. 146). As in this essay, Ellul always proclaims the definitively superior authority of the Revelation (p. 146) and demands that, for any work to be legitimate, it not exploit creation or serve only one's own happiness, but that it uniquely obey a vocation and render glory to God (p. 148). Though Ellul doesn't always specify it as the posture of the Reformers, all his theological works call for the same attitude that he claims for them here — that their sole effort was to express their fidelity to the Word and will of God, which is at the same time "both permanent, eternal, objective, identical with itself, and also present, innovative, subjective, and expressed *hic et nunc*" (pp. 148-49).

Some of the false gods that entice us from that fidelity are history and technique (pp. 149-50), the divinization of which Ellul elaborates in *The New Demons* (1973/75). The "Coda for Christians" at the end of that book is a strong rebuke urging Christians to stop demythicizing the Revelation in order to return to their work of desacralizing the contemporary myths. Ellul's comment here that modern painting and literature are witnesses to the way in which technique takes precedence (p. 150) is thoroughly justified in his full volume, *L'Empire du non-sens: L'Art et la société technicienne* (1980/not yet translated). Ellul's seemingly extravagant claims concerning the technicization of the arts are increasingly being substantiated by other social analysts, most notably Louis A. Sass in his book *Madness and Modernism: Insanity in the Light of Modern Art, Literature, and Thought* (New York: Basic Books, 1992). The translation of *L'Empire du non-sens* into English would be of tremendous benefit for us today, for in it Ellul shows the roots of the turn to the technological society that developed into the schizophrenic postmodernism that Sass documented in 1992.

In this article Ellul also mentions money (p. 150) as a power that was unleashed during the Reformation era. His ideas for desacralizing Mammon had already been thoroughly developed in 1952 in a lengthy article, "L'Argent" ("Money"), and then expanded in *Money and Power*

(1954, 1979/1984), which gives specific suggestions for desacralizing money, such as siding with human beings against money, not loving money or worrying about it, and profaning money by giving it away.

Though Ellul explains in this article the main difference between the society of the sixteenth century and that of the twentieth — that today's society is no longer basically religious, not fundamentally Christian — he concludes that very simply the problem now is still one of fidelity and obedience (pp. 151-53). This is a principal theme in *Prayer and Modern Man* (1971/70), which names obedience as the only discernible subjective and human motivation for prayer. There he explains that by obedience he does not mean duty or obligation, but an understanding of one's responsibility, of one's privilege to enter into the communion made possible by a God who loves us enough to command what sets us free.

As this article underscores, the importance of obedience is heightened by what seems the silence of God. Noting that the question for Israel, throughout the centuries of silence and absence in the course of their history, was how to maintain hope and fidelity, despite and against all reason, Ellul insists that this is our question, too (p. 153). The issue of persevering in faithfulness despite the circumstances is expounded in Ellul's *Hope in Time of Abandonment* (1972/73), which thoroughly displays the work of hope (not optimism) and nonconformity to which Christians are called in the face of the onslaught of technicization in our world.

Ellul's brief diatribe against traditional capitalism, with its escalation of useless production and incoherent distribution, with its immense injustice and inhumanity (pp. 153-54), is certainly needed today when it has even more "surpassed in volume and in density everything that existed before in leading astray what could have been a source of good for all." The same outrage is expressed in many of Ellul's sociological works, especially those on technology, but also in three articles that also expand themes previously noted in this chapter. "Technique and the Opening Chapters of Genesis" (1960/84) outlines Ellul's biblical foundation for his opposition to technique, objects primarily to the fallacies in the contemporary myth of work, and locates all the problems presently associated with work in the situation of sin. In "The Relationship Between Man and Creation in the Bible" (1974/84) Ellul mourns that human beings are destroying their own security by their present attitudes toward creation and calls those who believe in the Word of God instead to live within its limits. His article on "Work and Calling" (1974) reminds us that our particular Christian calling will be an entry into society's disorder and that our expression of vocation will upset the disorder further and call it into question.

That same task of questioning and upsetting our present society and summoning it to its proper limits is Ellul's directive in this chapter's article for combatting the hypocrisy of contemporary nationalism (pp. 154-55). His appeal for sustaining the state's secularity (pp. 155-56) compares to his frequent mandates for desacralization, as noted above.

Especially Ellul emphasizes here the singular vocation of Christians to remember that we are people of the Word and that for us the humble human word is invested with a unique gravity since it is the means by which the Revelation is heard; consequently, he urges us to be very rigorous in our use of words (p. 157). This criticism of the abuse of language and this petition for Christians to be disciplined in our employment of language were expanded into *The Humiliation of the Word* (1981/85), a book that is, I believe, one of Ellul's most important in light of the present postmodern derogation of language and meaning.

Ellul's similar admonition for Christians to be more demanding and more rigorous than the world on the subject of values (p. 158) and his criticism of the prodigious irrealism of the world's formulas (p. 159) anticipate *A Critique of the New Commonplaces* (1966/68), as well as his frequent and thorough calls for desacralization. This article's addition of the "American Way of Life" (with Ellul writing those words in English instead of French) to his list of sacral entities that clamor for our time, money, work, adoration, and all of our life (pp. 160-61) charges us to join the first Christians and the Reformers in refusing to sacrifice to the false gods of our times, to engage in the radical No to the sacralization of our world, and to follow the witness of the Reformers in their intentional fidelity to the only One who is not an idol (p. 161).

CHAPTER 7

"Christian Faith and Social Reality"

SOURCES

Ellul's beginning "Ladies and Gentlemen" and his final "I have spoken" remind us that the text of this chapter is a transcript of a conference presentation. Ellul continued to lecture, lead Bible studies, and preach through most of his life. In his final years, as a result of the strain of his wife Yvette's illness and death in 1991 and because some of his unpopular views on such subjects as AIDS, South Africa, and Islam put him out of favor in circles where he had been a prophetic spokesman, Jacques' own health failed and he became very discouraged.[1]

Since U.S. scholars could never hear Ellul unless they went to France (he refused to fly, though he traveled extensively throughout Europe and spent time in North Africa and Israel), this glimpse of his personality as a speaker is valuable.[2] The text reveals his passion for the task of

1. These glimpses of Ellul's final years were provided by Joyce Hanks, "Jacques Ellul, 1912-1994," and David Gill, "My Journey with Ellul," in the tribute issue of *The Ellul Forum* 13 (1994): 4 and 8-9, respectively.

2. The Association Jacques Ellul, based in France, has many audiotapes and videotapes of Ellul available, and Serge Steyer, the director of the French film *Jacques Ellul, l'homme entier*, is hoping to find funding to make an English-language version of the film. For further information or to become a member of the Association,

Christians, his insistence, his dogmatic overstatement to make a point. Though I have eliminated some of the rhetorical repetitions that overburdened the text, I have retained Ellul's run-on manner to give the flavor of his oral style.

Ellul gave another speech, on "Technique and Civilization," earlier at the same conference, and it was printed in the same volume of the *Free University Quarterly.* Since that speech emphasizes themes already introduced in this book, I chose instead to include this one, which provides some possibilities for Christian action that we have not previously seen.

We have already encountered the failures of some political and ecclesiastical activities in which Ellul had participated. It is important also to mention two of his most successful commitments. In 1958 he became actively involved with the youth in his home community of Pessac, a suburb of Bordeaux. In that year he and Yves Charrier founded one of the first clubs in France for the prevention of juvenile delinquency. Also, in 1968 Ellul joined an aspect of the environmental movement and served as president for a term of the "Committee for the Defense of the Aquitanian Coast," with which he combatted the government's plans to "develop" that area.

Although this transcription of Ellul's speech can be only a pale substitute for hearing Ellul speak in person, reading the following piece aloud — or, better yet, having someone read it to you with passion — may help you imagine how hearing these words from Ellul himself might have stirred you to act out your own Christian faith in the social realities that surround you.

---

contact Joyce M. Hanks, Department of Foreign Languages and Literatures, University of Scranton, Scranton, PA 18510-4646.

I must also add that Ellul's personality on a one-to-one basis was much different. Though his writings often seem harsh and hasty and careless, underneath lay a very gentle, hospitable man who did enormous research, read voluminously, and yet took time for interviews with graduate students such as myself. During our interview, his wife, Yvette, listened to the conversation, seemed to understand much of my English before it was translated for Jacques, and then served a lovely tea, with raspberries from the garden.

Christian Faith and Social Reality

Jacques Ellul

Ladies and Gentlemen,

Alas, I shall not be offering you solutions to the questions that we have been raising together during these few days. I will attempt only to open up the beginning of a possible path. And that could appear to you extremely thin, very weak, and yet I believe that if we do not accept such simple, such modest beginnings, there is very little chance that we shall get very far.

First I owe you an explanation for the title I have proposed: "Christianity[1] and Social Reality." Why did I not say "Social Problems"? Why did I not say "Society"? Why, in sum, have I said "Social Reality"? Social problems, insofar as, in France in any case, one could understand by that the problems of workers, the problems of the working class — that seemed to me to be a theme too much reduced. Not that I consider the problem of the working class as not very important, but I was attempting to think not of the working class alone but of the totality of the problems of our times, of our world, of our society.

On the other hand, if I said "society," "Christianity and Society," that allows us to avoid the real problems by falling into a doctrinal and general vision of the problem, into a theoretical vision,

1. Here Ellul says the word *christianisme*, whereas the printed title uses the phrase, *Foi Chrétienne*. The latter is what Ellul means. Throughout this article when Ellul says "christianisme," it will be translated "Christianity," to signify, not the institutional church or a social-cultural lifestyle, but the coherent faith stance for which "Foi chrétienne" stands in the title.

"Foi Chrétienne et Realité Sociale," *Free University Quarterly* 7, 2 (August 1960): 166-77.

into an abstract vision. We would talk then about society, and we could then pose the question of the individual and the society, or of Christianity and society in general. But what seems important to me is our [actual] society, the world in which we are living.

But I have been brought to the choice of this title for a more serious reason. It is that finally the term *social reality* obliges us to take seriously this term *reality* and brings us up against the division (but also the relationship) that was already familiar, was already the beginning of all [our] reflection — [namely,] the division and the relationship between *truth* and *reality*. Today we have completely forgotten this distinction. And we have forgotten it because science, in general, claims to bring us the truth. Now science agrees with reality finally. It is very important to learn again that truth and reality are not the same thing, that economic reality, historic reality, and scientific reality are not the truth; and inversely that the truth (as the idealists often would think) is not in itself a constraining force, an evident force, a certain force.[2] We all know this intellectual position, which consists in saying: one can do nothing against the truth, which will always triumph. I am not sure that the truth always triumphs; the lie has an extraordinary power. And the truth, if it is not brought to life by a human brain and human hands, has no force in itself. In other words, reality will never lead us to the truth, but the truth is nothing if it does not enter into a certain reality.

And this we must see in the perspective of the Christian revelation: the truth of God is first expressed in the Creation — that is, in the creation of reality; then, after what we usually call the Fall, there is a rupture between reality and truth; reality becomes independent of the truth of God; the meeting point of the truth of God in reality with the incarnation of Jesus Christ is the only point in all of human history where truth entirely penetrates reality.

And lastly, it is promised to us, for the end of time, that the truth of God will again take over the whole of reality, will penetrate

---

2. Up to this point I have translated Ellul's redundancies completely, to let stand the evidence that this is an oral presentation. For the rest of this article I will consolidate such phrases for the sake of more fluent reading. I will continue to use Ellul's run-on punctuation for the sake of preserving his tight connection of ideas — except when changes are necessary for the sake of clarity.

all reality, will reunite reality in God, in the moment, as Scripture tells us, "when God will be all and in all." So that when I pose the problem, the question of Christianity and social reality, I am simply posing the question of the relation *hic et nunc* between the truth of God and this temporal, momentary, local aspect of the reality that is our society. But we must take into consideration that the truth, this Christian truth, is not a doctrine, not a theology, not an immobile, abstract, and rigid truth; truth is the very power of the living God.

This is exactly the key of all that I shall go on to say. And the first step that we have to take as Christians, it seems to me, is to learn to look at social reality as it is, to see it as reality. That will seem a little thing. But it is very difficult to see the world that surrounds us as it is, the persons who are beside us as they are, neither more nor less, to avoid reducing this reality, for example, to a theory. I believe that Christians should always avoid making theories too general, which would enable them to explain everything easily, simply — a political theory or a philosophical theory that can demonstrate everything. I believe that we must never yield to a general theory of society, of the world, of history. Likewise, I believe that it will be necessary also to avoid refusing to see reality because it would be too terrible; that is a frequent attitude in our world. One refuses to look at what is, because involuntarily, unconsciously one steps back and says, "No, it is not possible for it to be like that; that would be too dreadful." Many intellectuals, for example, respond to every sociological analysis of the present human condition by saying simply, irrationally, "No, it is not possible," without any argument, without any serious attention.

Inversely, we should avoid regarding this reality as if it were nothing but desperate, nothing but perdition, demonization, marching toward a catastrophe, etc., and I think in that case of all the philosophies of the absurd, the philosophies of despair, the tendency of Sartrian existentialism, where one regards only the dark side, the negative side, and where one wants to see nothing else.

Accordingly, it is a matter of having an eye without prejudices, of being capable of seeing things as they are, with all their dimensions. Here we begin to encounter a great difficulty. The work of every specialist is to divide. We separate questions from each other and study one little piece at a time. Now when it is the issue of social reality, it is a matter of looking at it globally, synthetically, seeing the whole. And at this moment the task of the intellectuals becomes horribly difficult, because they are obliged to do political economy, sociology, social psychology, and to analyze technical phenomena, and to analyze intellectual techniques equally, and to look at everything at the same time. So to look at the whole instead of the little pieces demands a sort of conviction. And it is only in a synthetic vision of this kind that we have any chance of seeing what this social reality signifies.

We must also consider this social reality respectfully — that is, by accepting the facts as they are, without trying to squeeze them into an already-prepared framework, always being open to some new aspect that may show up. And there, isn't it, is the dogmatic position that I will criticize (not the dogma of theologians), which consists in having a truth all prepared, into which the facts must fit, and then refusing all the facts that will not coincide with your doctrine. I think for example of the attitude of the Marxists, who accept the facts that line up with their thought and who reject all the rest. Now, as surprising as this assertion may seem to you, I think that at present only Christians could meet the spiritual and psychological conditions for taking the attitude that I have just described. Only, it seems to me (despite all one could say against me about the dogmatic attitudes of Christians in the past, etc.), only Christians are able to look at the real and evaluate it, because they are not completely caught inside it, because they are connected to a transcendence that is not locked up in reality. And they are able, therefore, to step back for a certain distance, a certain perspective, to see this reality — being close to this world, but meanwhile not being of this world; already no longer belonging completely [to this world], they can have a certain independence. And they can also look at this world, as desperate as it is, as dark as it is, as worrisome as it is, because, properly, Christians find themselves in this extraordinarily privileged position; they have their hope elsewhere. Therefore, they need not conclude their discourse by saying to you, "It's terrifying, but nevertheless — nevertheless, it cannot possibly turn out so badly." Only the Christian can say to you, "It is terrifying, but *outside this reality, not*

171

within it there is the good and merciful will of God who manifested himself in Jesus Christ, because of which it is not over. The last word is not death and catastrophe."

Consequently this certainty, this hope, this conviction permits looking at tragic things as tragic. And inversely, Christians cannot render things more tragic than they are, cannot darken their description, cannot refuse to see all the elements of light and the positive elements that exist. First because they have no right to lead other people into a path of despair, and then because they must always remember that this world, this lost world, this social reality constantly marked by death is nevertheless the world to which God came, is nevertheless just this world, and not another, which God chose and which he loves.

And this, I believe, is the first step we have to take. It is a little thing. It is a little thing, to learn to see social reality as it is. But it seems to me to be of extraordinary importance, when we perceive that only a tiny number of people see it, this social reality, and that as a result most diagnoses that are pronounced over this society are inexact diagnoses. And so as a Christian, and as a Christian intellectual, I believe that our first work to do is to try to establish this exact diagnosis. This posture enables us to avoid three errors that are frequent, current, among Christians. First, as I have already insisted above, we should avoid making a Christian system, a Christian doctrine of the state, or of the economy, or of society. I think that there truly is not a Christian doctrine of any of them. There is a theology of power, there is a theology of the state in Scripture, of course, as [there is] a theology of work, for example, but it is not a matter of doing good theology by drawing out principles and by saying that now it suffices to apply those principles. I believe that this would be an error. It would be an error because one would, when all is said and done, remain on a purely intellectual level. In the present situation of our times, there is no chance of writing into political or economic reality a certain number of truths that would be drawn from a theology of the state or of the economy. And this is a temptation, in the biblical sense of the word, a diabolical temptation finally, to want to make a society that as society would be so-called Christian. It is a temptation because inevitably there is a chasm between the faith of people toward their savior and the creation of a certain number of institutions. To be Christian is an adjective that can be applied only to a human person; there are no Christian institutions because, finally, institutions cannot have faith in Jesus Christ. I don't believe there can be a Christian state; there are statesmen who are Christians, which is something else, but they will necessarily find themselves in the midst of political techniques, in the midst of political problems that are not Christian. And it is that which is our true situation, as persons converted by the spirit of God and sent into a world that to them remains the world and nothing but the world.

Thus the first error would be to make such a Christian doctrine of the state or of society.

The second error is exactly the opposite. It is to withdraw, the attitude that can be termed "pietist" and that consists in saying, "The world is terrible, the world is cursed, the world is lost, and consequently we leave it. We shall withdraw, we shall lead a purely spiritual life, and we'll let the world unravel itself as it wishes. Politics is the world of the demon; thus it has nothing to do with us." I believe that this also is an error, and a serious error, which leads the Church (I think for example of the problem of the Church in the people's republics) to accept a purely spiritual mission. The state accepts that there should be churches, that there should be preachers, even — if really necessary — that there be Sunday schools, on condition that this not entail any political, economic consequences in the work, in the attitude of the citizen, etc. This is the same problem that arose with Hitler. Now this, I believe, definitely pushes truth outside of reality, rejects the truth completely, which is exactly what we cannot accept.

And the third error consists in saying that the Church will enter into society, will become a constitutive element of this society, will ally itself with the authorities[3] and achieve an understanding between the spiritual power and the temporal powers (as the Catholic Church had done in Christendom). That is what we call the Con-

---

3. Ellul actually says "power" here, by which he means government. As we saw in his first major articles, he acknowledges the manifestation of the biblical notion of the principalities and powers when he writes or speaks of governmental authorities.

stantinian society, which claims more or less to prepare a kind of ascent, progress, of the society toward the kingdom of God. And I believe that there, too, there is an error, in a certain measure, because it all depends on a series of compromises. The Church accepts a certain number of disobediences by the state, and inversely, the state tolerates the presence of the Church, admits it in a corner of the society, sometimes with many honors, giving it what a French author called "a small folding-seat in the amphitheater."

But a witness to Jesus Christ cannot accept any compromise. And, to provide just a small example of the compromise in the era of Constantine, about ten years before Constantine decided to accept, to recognize the Christian church, a synod had declared that no Christian should render military service to Caesar and that he would be excommunicated if he did it voluntarily. One year after the recognition of the Church by Constantine, another synod declared that it was a duty to render military service to Caesar and that those who refused military service to Caesar would be excommunicated. Behold the kind of compromise to which one is inevitably drawn. Now, witnesses to Jesus Christ cannot accept any compromise; but at the same time they live in this world, have no right to place themselves outside it, no right to remain in the abstract; and they are consequently at once persons absolutely firm as witnesses to Jesus Christ but constantly engaged in new adventures in the midst of a world that will all the time demand of them to make compromises and to accept them.

The Church is certainly induced to participate fully in social reality, in the construction of the society, in its searching, but participating in this work in [the Church's] own way — that is, quite often in another way than the powers of the world would want. I could, then, summarize the problem which that poses as follows: on one side, the presence of the Church produces a certain tension in society; and on the other side, Christians are induced to pursue a particular action, a specific action — that is, an action that no one else but Christians could pursue in society.

Let us take up the two points again.

The Church, in the measure to which it bears the Word of God and testifies to the truth of God, creates a tension in relation to social reality, a tension that is not necessarily a conflict or a negation.

174

It is not a negative attitude, an attitude only critical; but the Church is induced to be at the same time a body that is on the earth, but that is nevertheless what Paul calls the body of Christ: both at the same time. In other words, it is on the one hand a sociological reality, but on the other hand it is not sociological; it is bound precisely to the head of the Church, who is in heaven. What can that signify concretely? Quite simply this: that in the measure to which the Church is present within a given social reality, it prevents this reality from closing in on itself, from withdrawing into itself. Quite simply because it belongs to reality on one side, but on the other reaches into eternity. And so it happens (and it is particularly essential in our society) that society cannot achieve its closure; society cannot accomplish its totality. Now our society is precisely a society that wants to close in on itself, that wants to be total if not totalitarian, that would control people in all their ins and outs, a society that would have mastery of the collective life and the individual life.

Now, Christianity prevents the accomplishment of this design of human beings for their society, and it is an accomplishment that would finally be mortal. Christianity maintains a breach in social reality, through which truth and freedom can penetrate. In this work the Church maintains one of the conditions for human life. It maintains among the powers a disequilibrium, but a creative disequilibrium. When it bears the Word of God, the Church is charged to maintain a disequilibrium among the different elements of society. Not in order to prevent society from doing what it thinks good, but to maintain a living current, to maintain a possible exchange among the different elements of a society.

Christianity takes the individual person seriously enough to affirm the necessity of a difference between one and others, to refuse a compact assimilation into a single bloc.

But on the other hand Christians are called to create within the society what no one else can do. There are a certain number of works, a certain number of tasks in which actually everyone is more or less involved today: that there are great movements for peace is very good; that there are great movements in order that disadvantaged peoples recover a sufficient level of life is very good; that there is a great movement so that the condition of the working class ceases to be proletarian is very good. But everyone today is convinced of

175

that; everyone agrees. So I will say: you needn't bother to be involved there, you needn't bother to be concerned for what everyone will do — here I am obviously thinking more of the small Christian minority in France; Christians in the Netherlands are much stronger, much more numerous, have many more means of action — since that will certainly happen anyway, you needn't bother to such a degree to blend into this whole mainstream. Let us rather try, as Christians, to think of the things that no one is doing, to see the problems that no one is seeing, and to tackle enterprises that are still completely unknown. I'll give some examples [of this great work]: desacralization.

We live in a world that, to the same extent that it more and more rejects the Christian faith, also fabricates for itself more and more idols, let's say, or myths, or false values. In the absence of true religions, we respond by creating values adapted to our religious need. And then the simple facts are transformed into religious values. For example, the state will be easily transformed into a religious value — or the nation, or progress, or work, or, in certain countries, socialism is transformed into a religious value. In other words, facts that, when they are nothing but facts, are perfectly acceptable, perfectly normal, become threatening and dangerous at the point when they are invested with sacral value. And I believe that Christians have an enormous service to render to humankind in smashing these idols. This is a watchword that Christians should always hear and that is always given to them by Scripture.

We are extremely satisfied because at the beginning our ancestors, the first Christians, smashed the pagan idols, that was a first point; and then, we other Huguenots are also very satisfied that in the sixteenth century our ancestors smashed the Catholic statues, that is a second point; but now there is more. There are no more statues to break, but there are always idols. Now I believe that by smashing the religious character of this or that or these facts we liberate human beings. We liberate them from their intellectual alienations and their spiritual alienations. We induce them to regard the world in which they live as a *reasonable world*. Thirty years ago one heard a lot of Christian preaching which said that the tragedy was rationalism, and Christianity should be the affirmation of the irrational. Alas, since then we have seen plenty of the irrational (for example, Hitlerism). The irrational is very dangerous. What characterizes people of our time is that they are not at all reasonable. On the contrary, they are perfectly irrational and unreasonable, and, as Christians, precisely we should remind them firmly that they must make modest but firm use of their reason: that the first step is that they must precisely not yield to dionysiac folly once they learn that they are not handed over to idols or to the powers, but that they live in a world which they must first regard as a reasonable world where things are only things. And that is all.

And this clarifies what I was saying about technique. Technique is what it is. Administration, as thing, is fine. The machine, as thing, is fine. But as soon as people put their faith in this machine, place all their hope in this machine, are convinced that their spiritual life depends on this machine and that actually the machine will be the vicarious instrument which will allow them cheaply to exercise love of neighbor, then at that moment we are in full idolatry. And that is what we have to destroy: to bring back the world of things exactly to be *only* things. And consequently a universe which certainly does not merit, for example, that we should sacrifice human beings to it. What is tragic is that once a thing has been transformed into a divinity, technique for example, we are ready to sacrifice persons to it. All the gods, we know from human history, have demanded human sacrifice. With Technique, with the State, with the Fatherland, that continues. If we regard the state as a set of offices, with a lot of papers, with typewriters — things — then we are much less ready to sacrifice the lives of human beings to it. Other reasons will be needed at that moment. The state is no longer the last reason. But at the same time, when we desacralize in this way, we are also rendering a service to humankind because problems become much more simple to resolve when they are simple reasonable problems and when we do not attach passionate and religious values to them. However, this kind of profanation of the divinities of modern people must be done not only in words, not in doctrines and in theories, but must also penetrate practice. If we want to profane the divinity of money, for Christians there is a simple means, and the Bible gives us only one, which is to give. You want your money to cease being a god, you have a means: give it. To profane the state, affirm the liberty of the person and your own liberty in actions — actions in the face of the decisions that can make an idol of the state. It might even mean, under certain conditions, refusing to participate in political life. I do not say always, all the time, but under certain conditions; sometimes to be a good, and true, and loyal citizen might mean refusing to play the game that the state offers us. Those are some examples very quickly.

Finally, one last task (and this still is only an example) that Christians can fulfill in our society is to try to build bridges, relations between people. We are living (all the sociologists now say it) in a society that is more and more partitioned, more and more divided, in classes, clans, professions, parties, and we know one another less and less. We speak our little languages; lawyers understand each other because they speak the same language, but they no longer understand anything that the doctors say, etc.

Obviously this is still more serious when we consider society as a whole. Now the very important role of Christians in our present society (of Christians because they are, as Peter says in his epistle, strangers and pilgrims on earth, because they are strangers and are called to go somewhere else) is precisely to restore the bonds, the communications between people, and especially between people who are enemies of one another. And that can be done only if Christians share the situations of these people, without sharing their myths, their beliefs, their ideologies. And then there is a constant give-and-take that Christians are called to establish. Involved with other people, with all other people, or the people of another clan, of another milieu, another group, in a common task, but still not committed totally, not one hundred percent, not for life and death, because they are bound to others. They are bound to their brothers and sisters in the Church.

How, indeed, can one build this bridge, these relations, among groups that do not know each other? Not theoretically, not by saying, "You know, you should contact your neighbor, you should show good will, that would be very good, that would be virtuous." That will convince no one. But unity among people can be established by the fact of the unity of the Church whose members must be involved in the milieux, and in the clans, and in the different parties. It is not by saying to workers, "It is not necessary for you to engage in the class struggle against your bosses," nor by saying to the managers, "You ought to be good bosses," that we can succeed in reducing the opposition between the classes. But what would be possible (I do not say that it is happening, and when it does not happen it is the Church's betrayal) is that workers, because they believe in Jesus Christ, and bosses, because they believe in Jesus Christ, find themselves truly, totally united in the fellowship of the saints within the Church. Then, there, there would be a true encounter. And this is an example of what we should try to do. [It is] exactly the same problem when it is a matter of political parties. I don't think that it is very successful to have a Christian party that lumps together all Christians. I believe rather that the role of Christians is to be with the other people. That is, it seems important to me that in all the parties (including even the communist party) there should be Christians and that the role of these Christians should be to be well in tune with and serious comrades for those who are in the same party, but that they unceasingly remember, *and that is the significance of their political commitment,* that they are more united with their brothers in Jesus Christ who belong to the opposite party than with their comrades of the same party.

It is this unity of the Church sending its members everywhere that can reduce oppositions in society, that can bring back people who no longer understand each other to understand one another [again] by the intervening of Christians. These have been two small examples of possible works. I am devoted to beginning from a precise theological given, and then to describe, not a plan for a general reform of society, but rather tasks in which we as Christians can be involved right now.

It is not a matter, then, of preparing a sort of ascension of society toward the kingdom of God. It is not a matter of beginning on earth a kingdom of God that will finally end in heaven. It is a matter of something more modest, and, I believe, biblically more true. It is a matter of being within practical social reality the sign, simply the sign (and not the beginning), not more than a sign, but in any case the sign that points to the truth, the sign that there is this truth, and that we are not marching toward this truth, that we shall not attain this truth at the end of our long pilgrimage, because this truth comes to us, it is the truth that travels; it is not that we travel toward truth; this truth advances toward us, this eschatological truth illuminates us, already now in its movement that approaches us and our reality. And it is of that [truth] that we are to be the sign now for the people of this time.

I have spoken.

TRAJECTORIES

Perhaps the most significant idea in this article on "Christian Faith and Social Reality" is Ellul's profound distinction between reality and truth (p. 169), which undergirds the whole argument of *The Humiliation of the Word* (1981/85). That book expands his comment here that science, economics, and history all claim to be true, but are, in fact, of the order of reality since the fall. This speech, however, is perhaps the best summary in the entire Ellul corpus of his definitions of reality and truth and of the implications of that distinction for how Christians can see reality (pp. 169-72).

His remarks reveal again much of Ellul's understanding of his own task — to show the whole (for example, of the technological society), to face the reality clearly (in what might seem to be brutal sociological analysis), and yet to know hope (usually offered by him in a related theological work in order not to water down the rigor of his social criticism). Consequently, he criticizes dogmatism that claims to have a ready-made truth (p. 171). The example that he cites of Marxism and the contrast he makes with the perspective and independence of Christians is greatly elaborated in *Jesus and Marx: From Gospel to Ideology* (1979/88), which criticizes socialist "Christianities" that lose that independence by conforming to a materialist ideology.

Ellul again provides one of his best summaries when he outlines the three errors Christians must avoid — namely, making a Christian system or doctrine of the state or the economy (since *Christian* is an adjective that can be applied only to human beings); a pious retreat from the world; or entering unquestioningly into a Constantinian society that claims to be making progress toward the kingdom of God, which leads to compromises (pp. 173-74). One or more of these errors is expounded in almost all of Ellul's ethical works, but most especially in *False Presence of the Kingdom* (1963/72), published just a few years after this speech.

We have already noted in earlier chapters Ellul's proposal that the presence of the Church should instead establish a tension in its relation to society, a breach in the social reality by which truth and freedom can penetrate (pp. 174-75), and his crusade that Christians do the work of desacralization (p. 175). Often, as in this speech, Ellul contends that only Christians can do this — which seems a typical overstatement to make his point that one must be free from the idols in order to explode their myths. Certainly he is right to emphasize this as an important task for Christians, but is he equally wrong (as critics contend) to insist that it is exclusively theirs? Indeed, others are able to point out false values and myths in the society around them, even as other groups can work for peace — but Ellul proceeds to justify the overstatement by reiterating his critique that the modern world must learn that it is not free from the idols and the powers (pp. 176-77). The entire first part and some later sections of *The Ethics of Freedom* (1973, 1975/1976) expound this idea of the emancipation of human beings from enslavement to the powers as that is possible only in the redemption of Christ and the freedom he made possible by his triumph over the powers.

A third task — and here Ellul does overstate his case by saying that only Christians can do this — is to try to establish bridges, relationships between people and especially those who are enemies (p. 178). This challenge is without doubt desperately needed today, when we live in a society more and more partitioned, divided not so much by occupations but by small interests and victimization mentalities, *our* separate jargons almost forty years after Ellul spoke some of these phrases. However, his emphasis that the ability to do this bridge-building comes from being attached to the community of the church is one idea that Ellul did not develop very well in his corpus. Perhaps this was because his own experiences with the institutionalized church were frequently not good. Whatever the reason, Ellul must be criticized for inadequate attention to building the Christian community. Nonetheless, his notion of the presence of Christians in all the parties and unified among themselves to draw others together (pp. 178-79) is an idea badly needed in our age of political mayhem.

Ellul closes his speech with the call for Christians to be the sign — simply the sign, no more than a sign, but certainly the sign — that truth comes toward us (pp. 179-80). At the conclusion of *Hope in Time of Abandonment* (1972/73), Ellul seems to contradict himself by saying that Christians can't be a sign, since the sign they offer would be lost amid all the other signs of present society. That book was written partly to counteract misunderstandings of his emphasis on Christian presence in the world. Elsewhere in the book he does affirm that Christians are a sign of hope. And in *The Ethics of Freedom*, which was written slightly later (1973, 1975/1976), he once again develops

182

the notion that Christians do not claim to be the kingdom of God, but live as a sign of its truth.

The three articles of this chapter and Chapters 3 and 5 challenge contemporary Christians to be **realists, reformers,** and **creators of tensions** in response to the situation of the world under the influence of the principalities and powers. As we have seen throughout this book, Ellul himself fulfilled these roles in his various genres of writing. His works of social criticism exposed the reality of the world by questioning the illusions of politics, economics, and other social factors. His biblical explications created tensions by pointing to the truth that is an alternative to the world under the influence of the powers. Finally, he sought in his ethical works to reform contemporary Christianity, to call it back to its fundamental tasks of serving as a sentinel and as a sign of the truth of the kingdom of God.

CHAPTER 8

"Innocent Notes on
'The Hermeneutic Question'"

SOURCES

We have already encountered (in the introduction of Chapter 5) Ellul's description of how his intensive honoring of the Revelation began and how he was *seized* by a text that became "Absolute Truth" for him, a "living contemporary Word" that he "could no longer question." This chapter shows the major implication of that reverence for the Revelation in Ellul's convictions concerning methods for interpreting the Scriptures.

It is essential to recognize the irony of both halves of Ellul's title. By putting the words *the hermeneutic question* in quotation marks, Ellul signals that his inquiry will raise doubts about this hackneyed phrase. We will see in the following essay that he confronts the theological establishment head-on and questions its jargon.

Ellul's definition of his notes as "innocent" is doubly wry. His comments are not naive or unsophisticated. This symbolic modesty is an indirect invitation to be taken seriously. On the other hand, though his remarks are frank, they certainly are not innocuous or inoffensive. If he intends the word *innocent* to mean "righteous" or "virtuous," that would be a sentiment with which many laypeople who think the theologians have stolen the Bible from them would agree; many members of the academic guild, on the other hand, would resent the judgment that might make on their work. Though Ellul published this piece thirty years ago, the issues it raises still buzz in the halls at the annual meeting of the American Academy of Religion/Society of Biblical Literature.

Ellul himself did not receive a graduate degree in theology, but he did complete everything except the thesis. The thoroughness of his own research dispels any suspicion that he is unstudied. For example, in *Reason for Being: A Meditation on Ecclesiastes,* Ellul noted that he "slogged through the Hebrew text. Nine different translations helped, and kept me in check." Furthermore, "it involves my cultural background and my knowledge. Over the years I have read some books and articles on Ecclesiastes, including those by W. Vischer, J. Pedersen, W. Lüthi, and G. von Rad." All these are footnoted, and then he goes on to mention and footnote seven more major scholars on the book. Other comments in his introduction, structural analyses, and footnotes reveal the enormous exploration that undergirded his reflections. Yet, though he did not read texts simplistically, Ellul still claimed in the "Preliminary, Polemical, Nondefinitive Postscript" that begins *Reason for Being* this "innocent" approach to what he considered "the Revelation":

> I am no scholar or exegete, neither interpreter nor theologian. My only qualification is that I have read, meditated on, and prayed over Ecclesiastes for more than fifty years. I have probably explored it more than any other book in the Bible. . . . We could say that I am now committing this dialogue to writing.[1]

In the following article Ellul combines the insights of a cultured person conversant with linguistic theory and the "innocent" forthrightness of a resolute believer. To highlight the latter, I have retained Ellul's capitalization and addition of the definite article for "the Revelation of God," for that has a great significance for him, which is unfolded in this article. To make Ellul's argument easier to follow, the reader is encouraged to remember that the terms *signifier* and *signified* (and also *signification*) will be used to explain Ellul's formal linguistic terms, *signifiant* and *signifié.*

---

1. Jacques Ellul, *Reason for Being: A Meditation on Ecclesiastes,* trans. Joyce Main Hanks (Grand Rapids: William B. Eerdmans, 1990), pp. 2 and 1.

Innocent Notes on "The Hermeneutic Question"

Jacques Ellul

For the profane,[1] [who is] neither theologian nor philosopher, the hermeneutical problem seems to be posed simply enough: evidently we must begin with the rejection, with which one easily agrees, of the theopneustia [i.e., God-breathedness, a literal echo of II Tim. 3:16]. The men who wrote the biblical text were only men, and even inspired by God, they remained men. They have consequently apprehended the Revelation of God with their conceptual apparati; they understood it by means of their images, their stereotypes; they transmitted it with their language. It is a matter of discovering, beyond their language, their symbols, and their concepts, what they had heard and received, since our language and our conceptual apparati are no longer the same: this appears *self-evident*. And that observation is linked to a second one: the Revelation took place in the form of a *word* addressed by God to these men. But they wrote it down. What is transmitted to us is dead, stiff writing. There is work to be done to restore to it life, vigor, presence — that is, to make it become again a word challenging human beings, which the written text does not do. And when we will have rediscovered that

1. Ellul uses this word *profane* ironically, to signify laypersons and thereby to jar us at the outset — even as the title did — to recognize that this article will question many of the common assumptions of the academic guild about hermeneutical issues. In the few places where Ellul uses the word *profane* in this way, I have retained it and added quotation marks to highlight Ellul's intended critique of those who denigrate laypeople's "simplistic" reading of the Bible.

'Notes innocentes sur la 'question herméneutique,'" L'Evangile, hier et aujourd'hui: Melanges offerts au professeur Franz J. Leenhardt (Genève: Editions Labor et fides, 1968), pp. 181-90.

"beyond" of their language, of their images, of their knowledge, we need to translate it into *our* language, to regrasp it with our conceptual apparati, to translate it into the images and the symbols of our times. To simple eyes, that is what the hermeneutical question seems to be, and it imposes itself with a blinding obviousness. It goes without saying. As a nonspecialist Christian,[2] I have been asking myself for years if, finally, it is as true as it is obvious.

*   *   *

To confront this problem, we ought not to react as many Christians have tried to, by referring to the Holy Spirit. We easily confuse [different] questions.

When ancient theologians elaborated the doctrine of the Holy Spirit, they were not trying to resolve what we today call the hermeneutical problem, but rather were seeking to know how a human word can become truth, how the biblical text (understood) is invested with a signification that I receive as true. But the biblical text must be humanly understood.[3] If indeed the biblical text containing revelation transmitted nothing to my intelligence, we could purely and simply do without it: it would be useless, and we could fall back on the Revelation direct from the Holy Spirit, without any need for the objective support this revealed and written word constitutes. The text has to have a humanly discernible significance for there to be any possibility for the Holy Spirit to transform what is signified into truth. In summary, to use modern vocabulary, it is not the movement from the signifier to the signified that is the work of the Holy Spirit (no more than the movement from Scripture to the Word [in the Barthian sense]) but rather the transformation of the signified into truth. There is thus a dichotomy to be observed, and it is legitimate at the first phase to treat the text like a human document to be interpreted. To consider the biblical text as a human

2. Again we notice Ellul's irony. Even though he did not receive a graduate theological degree, he was enormously well read theologically — as we saw in Chapter 5, for example, with his awareness of Paul Ramsey's work within a year of its publication.

3. In other words, the Holy Spirit does not bypass the problem.

187

document was already the claim of historians since the eighteenth century, but by now we have advanced by a great step: previously the question had been its relation to fact, and today the question is its very meaning. So the situation is much more radical. But if it is thus, then we need to establish a general hermeneutics, valid for all texts, and even for all signs, and biblical hermeneutics would be only one particular case of this common science of interpretation.

*   *   *

Actually, this way of posing the hermeneutical problem today (and we will need to reflect on this "today"!⁴) seems (once again to the "profane"!) to rest upon four presuppositions, admitted as certain verities by everyone, and for this reason never demonstrated, never critiqued. The four presuppositions go in pairs. The first consists in this: On the one hand there is the adequacy of the human language on the biblical cultural level (i.e., that the language in which the biblical authors wrote the revelation was in fact really the ordinary, daily language of their times). On the other hand, the myths that express (signify) what was revealed had a historical-cultural character (i.e., that the myths were the normal expression of the intellectual milieu in which the biblical authors were living, their cultural means of expressing their thought).

The second pair is antithetical: on the one hand, there is the inadequacy of the language of the contemporary Christian message, on the cultural level (i.e., that the biblical language we use no longer transmits anything); on the other hand, there is a radical devaluation (resulting from the new thought modes of our present mental universe) of the biblical myths as a signifier of the revealed signified.

And these two pairs of antithetical presuppositions themselves rest on two basic "postulates": primitive thought takes a mythical

---

4. Ellul's exclamation point might suggest ironically that the emphasis on contemporaneity is not so important as is claimed, or perhaps he is underscoring the need for the work (which extensively characterized his own long career) of reflecting on the nature of contemporary society in the light of the principalities and powers, an idea that he introduced in his earliest major articles (see Chapters 1 and 2). Indeed, in *The Ethics of Freedom*, Ellul's section on hermeneutics follows his section on the powers.

form, and modern thought is rational. The entire system is coherent; the *entire* hermeneutical problem actually rests on that. These postulates are self-evident. Now, I propose that we should be suspicious of the self-evident. For a long time we have abandoned Lévy-Bruhl's conception of primitive thought.[5] But here we are dealing with a mode of thought that lasted until the eighteenth century. Now I suggest that well before that there were schemas, modes of thought, conceptual apparati [that were] perfectly rational: consider the engineers' school at Alexandria that trained Archimedes. Everything we know about it indicates that here there was a century of rational thought, rigorously scientific, and making no concessions to the mythical. Or look now a few centuries later at Roman juridical thought: there is nothing more rigorous, more cut-and-dried, more exact than this analysis of social relations, based on perfectly articulate methods. And don't say that these are merely exceptions . . . On the one hand, [these instances] could be multiplied, and on the other, these jurists were perfectly understood, in their formulations and their solutions, by the inhabitants of the Empire. Thus their rational thought was not obscure. Inversely, it is rather audacious to pretend that modern people have become rational: the people who consult tens of thousands of fortune-tellers and diviners, for whom the rubric of the horoscope is one of the most important, who gamble madly, who go along with all the publicity and propaganda, whose basically irrational motivations are exploited by the advertisers, etc., are not rational or scientific people at all. They accept a thousand new religious forms; they enter into all the myths proposed to them. They live in a technicized universe as beings obsessed with magic. I therefore believe that the classical antithesis is inexact, and that there have always been mixtures of the rational and the irrational, of the mythical and the logical, of the experimental and the subconscious . . . with diverse proportions and forms, but never with disqualifications such that communication and the significance of it would become impossible.

5. Lucien Lévy-Bruhl (1857-1939), French philosopher, dedicated much of his life to studying primitive societies and concluded that the primitive mentality, in contrast to the civilized, was pre-logical and based upon a principle of participation (i.e., that any thing or person can be both itself and something other than itself).

But going on from there, I am obliged to question again the four presuppositions indicated above. I do not have the space in these brief pages to demonstrate at length the inexactitude of each of these propositions. Let us briefly review them. Without doubt, the biblical authors apprehended the Revelation of God with their own conceptual apparati. But we are talking of *Revelation* and of *God;* it is easy to understand that this relationship would necessarily turn upside down these apparati! Without which we would consider that we have to do with a simple inert object, which people could express to their liking. Accordingly (but it is necessary to *believe* that in this matter it is truly *God revealing himself*), the customary language and the myths that constitute the signifier are modified, and often profoundly. The biblical authors no longer speak the language of everyone and of every day; their language is no longer on the nondescript cultural level of their time: without doubt this level serves as the point of departure, the base, but the language is changed to the point of glossolalia. The customary myths are radically invested with new forms and meanings: they still belong by their structures to the historical-cultural landscape, but they are disconnected from it by the use God makes of them, by virtue of a new signified. Consequently (and a hundred biblical texts of the Old and New Testaments show it and are in the memories of everyone), this language, these myths, quite far from being the common vehicle at that moment, would become a source of incomprehension, of misunderstandings, of ruptures of communication between the bearer of the Revelation and the people around him. In other words, there was no adequacy of language on the part of biblical authors at the average level of communication in their times. And on the other hand, the myths utilized are so strongly charged with a new signified, that the latter transcends by far the primitive historical-cultural character of these myths. Consequently, it was not easier for the contemporaries of Isaiah or of Jesus to understand what they were saying than for our contemporaries. And using the same language, the same myths, inserting [them] into an apparently identical mental structure was to the contrary an additional source of confusion.

The second pair of presuppositions is equally inexact. It is not because the cultural milieu has changed that the Christian message is transmitted in an inadequate language; this inadequacy does not seem evident to me (except on the totally superficial and uninteresting level of the use in our translations of words [that were] current in the eighteenth century and that have aged — that is, "mercenary" for "worker"). For the words of this Christian language are charged with images and meanings by their long use, and if they are not theologically exact for everyone (this has always been the case), it is false [to say that this makes them] words without content. They are rather, most often, words of current language (grace, love, hope, faith, etc.) that are no more incomprehensible today than before. As for the devaluation of the biblical myths because of the rational character of modern human beings, that seems to me entirely illusory. Science can contest this or that biblical explanation, but that does not appear to me more serious than the contesting of this same explanation by Greek philosophy or by Buddhism. It is not the recognition of scientific accuracy on one point that brings with it the coherence of the personality around this scientific knowledge; people can have very well understood scientifically what is the phenomenon of death, and [still] continue to be afraid of it, and thereby can construct a set of myths on the subject. Or else they can understand this phenomenon *in another dimension* and consequently accept the word of the Revelation. When will they admit, in the hermeneutical debate, this observation, recognized by all the psychologists, that people are not beings all of one piece and coherent in themselves?

*   *   *

But we need to go much farther: we have said that the biblical myths are the signifier of a signified (revealed to faith). We must admit that if God is God, what is revealed does not vary essentially. It is the same yesterday, today, tomorrow.

Then what matters is to know if the existence of what is permanently revealed does not give to the signified a certain power, an orientation, finally a second meaning, which renders it perceptible through the signifier for those who believe what is revealed. In other words, [we must ask] whether what is revealed does not create a much greater possibility of comprehension between contemporary

191

Christians and Christians of the first century than the identity or non-identity of the signifier. At the very most the supposed inadequacy of the signifier would add a supplementary difficulty, but not at all a decisive one. But this position is derived from an inversion of the habitual process. Generally one says: a signifier is transmitted to us that permits us to receive and understand a signified — supposing this path that leads from the signifier to the signified, and an independence of one from the other. Now, I think that the dimension of the Revelation (which I am quite obliged to admit as a Christian!) changes this process: what dominates is the Revealed [One], which posits a certain signified that determines a certain signifier. I therefore have to begin with the Revealed [One] to understand the signifier. It serves nothing to say that it is nevertheless the signifier that enables me to hear the Revealed [One]: no, at the most it is the signified. But in any case I understand nothing of it, whatever be the signifier, if I do not receive and believe the Revealed [One]. And, on the other hand, that implies a union between the signified and the signifier: I cannot choose any one signifier to fit that particular signified. And I cannot then get rid of "metaphysical" (?) myths,[6] concepts from biblical times, as if they were purely cultural, nothing more. I well know that I will be told, "You are talking here about the relationship between the believer today and the believer of the past. But what interests us in the hermeneutical question is the relationship between believer and unbeliever." First of all I believe that this is not entirely exact, for in this genre of research it is always a matter of showing that the biblical texts do not transmit to us the exact contents of revelation for faith. That is always the first step. In the second place, I believe that this is a misapprehension on the part of the hermeneuts: indeed, in this genre of research it is most often a question of the preaching of the message; the intent is to discover (by means of hermeneutics) the message in order to announce it to the nonbelievers in a language that might be accessible to them. Now, this is to expect far too much from hermeneutics. If the message comes from the Revelation of God, hermeneutics can uniquely make the text more clear to me,

6. Pastor Charles suggests that Ellul adds the question mark after the term *metaphysical* to join in the Barthian criticism of the demythologizing of Bultmann.

but it can never make it true for me, and it will never make me grasp this message. Therefore, as far as unbelievers are concerned, it permits them only to understand this text logically, rationally, but not at all to receive its message.[7] It will thus not be hermeneutics that will allow the modern unbeliever to have even the least access to the meaning of what is revealed. Now, it is that alone which should matter for a Christian. And it is just this concern that has led many along these paths, but I believe that they are paths that lead nowhere. IF, for faith, the biblical text contains (not in its totality, nor in its plenitude, nor in an obvious way, that goes without saying!) the truth of the Revelation, IF the latter cannot be known by any other way than this text, which itself exists only in accordance with the truth that is Jesus Christ and in referring to him, IF we cannot know Jesus Christ except by means of the Bible, hermeneutics will never deliver to me, as method, the signified of this text, for it is not apt to discern the truth. The decisive point is that by faith *I know* that this Bible *has* a signified, and that the latter *is* truth. Faith *in* Jesus Christ makes me add faith *to* this text. Most certainly there can be misunderstandings concerning interpretation; there can be problems posed about how Jesus Christ is known by this way, but that remains radically secondary, the decisive question being that of the faith which makes me affirm the existence of a true signified. And consequently the path here too, as before, is the inverse of the one that we conceive humanly: instead of saying, "one goes from the signifier to the signified and ultimately from there to the truth," I already said above, "we go from the signified to the signifier." And now we must add, "we go from Jesus Christ the truth to the signified."

*   *   *

7. [Ellul's footnote:] I constantly maintain in these lines the term "biblical text," for I think that there can be no grasp of revelation but tied to this text. I indicated earlier a first reason. Further, if we let go of this text the least little bit, the message that we claim to announce will necessarily be a kind of philosophical thought; it will be about principles, about a metaphysic, or else a declamation *above* the history of salvation: only permanent reference to the text can maintain that it is about a history. Letting go of the text by means of hermeneutics is the major betrayal that transforms the history of God with human beings into a theory.

However, I was saying that there can be misunderstandings on interpretation . . . and I know well that at this point the hermeneuts reclaim their authority: "We never claimed to do more than resolve some secondary problems. The 'how' of the relation of signified-signifier, the 'how' of deciphering, etc." It is quite certain that hermeneutics can bring down human obstacles, and establish a more exact meaning. But it is research of the same genre as the enterprise undertaken a century ago by the historians who were trying to establish by scientific means which were the words undoubtedly pronounced by Jesus . . .[8] For just at the moment when [that research] resolves these difficulties, it amasses others. There is no intellectual question more difficult that those raised by this method: when all is said and done, the text becomes much less clear and accessible when it is approached from this angle. On the one hand there is the great danger of the rupture between the signifier and the signified, to which I have already alluded. There is the postponement of the possibility of a message to the moment when finally a hermeneutic will be possible. There is the dilution of the situation of human beings before God in the play of endless mirrors where every image points toward another and where one can never grasp anything but images. There is the uncertainty proceeding from this reality never encountered but only seized by . . . and it is always a relation of a relation. There is then the triumph of the subjectivities. Subjectivity of the witnesses who are never anything more than witnesses to some kind of accident, to which is added the subjectivity of the narrators and over which plays the subjectivity of the transcriptors. What do we grasp? This leads us naturally to the primacy of horizontal relations, and to the affirmation that finally there is never anything but human beings talking to human beings. The greater the intended rigor of the hermeneutical method, the more it leads to evacuating the vertical God-humankind relation, and to the negation of a possibility for the reality of what is revealed.

*   *   *

8. The contemporary proliferation of studies in the "Third Quest for the Historical Jesus" makes Ellul's comments here particularly relevant.

But if the problem of hermeneutics is so acute today, it is because it rests upon a crisis of language. Language is itself in question. We know innumerable works on the analysis of language today, the utilization of linguistics by the structuralists, the conclusion of a kind of autonomy of language that ends by having its specific life, almost independently, one could say, of the one who speaks and who is merely "haunted by language." Now, I would want to underline that this questioning of language, this analysis, this discussion of meaning, all of this is not an invention, not a creation of eminent thinkers, who make this incredible progress in the critique of humankind, and in becoming aware, audacious to the point of plumbing what is the most lively and indispensable to human beings (communication): actually we are in the presence of the simple reflection of a real crisis. Language no longer signifies anything in our society. And that comes from very precise sociological phenomena that I cannot detail here: abuse of language in advertising, propaganda, gigantesque logorrhea of information, mixing thousands of insignificant informational bits with one or two significant ones, permanent tautology and redundancy of messages of all kinds (political, scientific, etc.), banalization of communication, disconnection of the spoken and the speaker, the appearance of the specific language of machines, etc. It is in this context of the *factual* annihilation of language that the critique and the intellectual analysis made of it are situated. And it is within the prolongation of those (intellectual) problems of language (but it is wrong to regard the tired, fading, meaningless language of our epoch as *the* language . . . as if it had always been the same!) that the hermeneutical problem is located. The latter [the hermeneutical problem] is explained only by the former [the annihilation of language]. Now, ultimately the analysis by specialists in language leads to two final conclusions or observations: on one side a sort of autonomy of language, which forbids saying for example, "I am speaking" — one goes on more and more to formulate it thus, "The word speaks" or "Language speaks" or else "It speaks." It is no longer I who speak but some "it" through me. Innumerable novels reflect this thought: a word unhooks itself, unrolls itself, empties itself . . . there is no longer a subject speaking, there is no difference between the diverse personages who express themselves; it speaks. [Speech is happening.]

195

And in the same way in how many poems do we see the poet insisting on the autonomy of language . . . The second conclusion that one can draw from these analyses is actually the disappearance of the signified. There remain some signs, a signifier that we can grasp, study, but at the limit it is not sure that there is anything more: language speaks of language and refers to itself. Following these two types of study and these two antithetical positions, we see for example Lefebvre[9] and Legrand reaching the same conclusion: the former begins with the refusal of this situation in the name of a Marxist humanism, concludes that the entire modern discussion of language winds up with the disappearance of sense. The second is a specialist in the analysis of language and follows the research, for example, of the "Stuttgart Group" with Bense, on the language of machines . . . But he concludes with this question: "Why bother to save language when one no longer has anything to say, *when there is no longer anything to say?*" That is the end of the line.

*   *   *

But then do we really have to accept going to work to rethink the biblical text in accordance with this research and these analyses, based on this sociological crisis of language? Of course that will be very exciting; that could seem a duty (not to reject the question that science puts to us!). Unfortunately, I am not sure that we have to accept whatever question proceeds from a reflection provoked by the situation. For if I believe in Jesus Christ, I am by that very fact bound to the existence of an "I" and of a signified. It is not true that "it" speaks. There is an "I" who speaks. The God of Jesus Christ. And everything derives from that. I am obligated here to formulate a judgment of truth and error. And in the face of the *observation* that, in our society, anonymity is growing, I must refuse to elevate this "One" [an abstraction of the God who speaks] to the status of scientific truth. Anonymity is a lie and an alibi. It is not true that the speech speaks: it is God who speaks the Word that he addresses to me. For that is what Jesus Christ teaches me. Nor can

9. Lefebvre probably means Lucien, the father of the main French school of historiography. The rest of the names mentioned in this discussion are untraceable.

I accept any more the disappearance of the signified: this word is addressed to me to tell me "something."

The fact that in modern society words no longer say anything, that language becomes a simple structure, I cannot consider as a normative fact, but as a consequence of . . . I'll go on to say, ashamed: sin.

But faith in Jesus Christ teaches me that the word has a meaning, and that I receive in the Revelation a signified. Here again I have to pronounce a judgment of truth and error. And I must reject, on the grounds of faith, everything that tends to erase the "I" who speaks (as with the simplistic projects of Robinson[10]) and the true signified. And moving on from there I have to proceed to the criticism of the exterior phenomenon.[11]

*   *   *

I well know that the extremists of the tendency I am contesting will say, "But what are all these words that you are using: Revelation, faith, God, etc.; what do they mean?" One could respond with many things. First of all they themselves use, without embarrassment, words like "Speech" or "It" or "Signified" . . . and they have the air of knowing what that means . . . But there is more: I will say that in fact they already know very well the meaning of the words in the face of which they pretend to be innocent.[12] And it is precisely because they know it that they act as if they ignored [their meanings], for [they are aware that] these terms are very embarrassing for their system. And finally if they genuinely ignore it [the meaning of the "God" terms], this means that they are the prisoners of the

10. Since this article was published in 1968, Ellul probably refers to *Honest to God* by Bishop J. A. T. Robinson (Philadelphia: Westminster Press, 1963). Note again that Ellul was not "innocent" of what was happening on the theological scene throughout Europe and the U.S.A.

11. Ellul's "there" means the truth of the divine "I" who speaks; the "exterior phenomenon" that he must critique probably refers to the emptying of language described several paragraphs earlier. Ellul critiqued this emptying of language in numerous articles and especially his book *The Humiliation of the Word.*

12. Ellul is delightfully ironic here, using the same word as in his title. Both are a feigned ignorance.

neo-dogmatism of language in which one is limited indefinitely to work on syntax. And then I will say that as Christians we must deliberately come out of the syntagmatic prison where they want to confine us, in order for us to fall back on semantics, which alone is coherent with an attitude of intellectual humility before the Bible.[13] In this way, they [the extremists] will understand the meaning of those famous words [that are supposed to be] so obscure . . .

*　　*　　*

In faith we receive a consistent signified — a signified that by its very existence denies the contemporary analysis of language, a signified that imposes itself on the language and that rejects the crisis of language, and, in so doing, rejects the proposed hermeneutic itinerary. It is absolutely vain to proceed in the apparently logical fashion of saying that this signified is only known by means of the text, and consequently . . .[14] For it is indeed permissible to treat the biblical text like any other document, but we are sure in this way never to grasp *anything*. I do not say to grasp a little something that would be the basis of a possibility for faith. I say *nothing*. Indeed, either the biblical text is bearer of the Revelation or not. It is a predecision of faith or of unbelief. But from the viewpoint of faith, what can be grasped by means of a lay hermeneutic is nothing since it is not the central object, the goal, the real content, the hidden sense, the life-giving spark of the text. At the most one can glean a few good fragments for an archaeological museum of thought or of civilizations. But then if in this biblical language there is a signified that is not intrinsic but extrinsic to it [i.e., not reducible to the words], recognized by faith and given to faith, this means as a second step that there is not a general hermeneutic valid for the biblical text and of which biblical interpretation would be a partic-

13. "Syntagmatics" refers to structuralist methodology. This will be a constant theme in Ellul's later works on language: that semantics, the science of meaning, is good; contrarily, syntagmatics, a preoccupation with language games for their own sake, is bad.

14. Ellul probably means that this phrase, which trails off, would continue, "consequently there can be no solid meaning." Usually Ellul uses ellipses to force the reader to finish the sentence or think of other examples.

ular case. There is a specific biblical hermeneutic, different from the others, for which faith is the condition of its existence and of which the method is given by the biblical text itself. I believe that the Christian must yield to this "limitation," in ceasing to cast longing eyes toward that intellectual exterior, seemingly more fascinating, intelligent, seductive. We must accept the specificity of the text witnessing to the Revelation, and accordingly the method that is relevant to it. And in particular that the famous problem of the Word that becomes dead by the fact of being Scripture is, in this situation and in this perspective, a false problem.

These are the reflections of simple common sense by a non-specialist, but I once learned that the universal priesthood qualifies every last one of the faithful to participate in the common ministry of the Church, including that of the Word . . .

TRAJECTORIES

Ellul's closing remarks about his participation in the priesthood of all believers throws the gauntlet to the academic guild. His "innocent notes" stubbornly question the general assumption of many academics that our language and conceptual apparati are radically different from that in which the Revelation of God is recorded (pp. 186-87).

Ellul shows both the influence of Barth and Kierkegaard and working knowledge of standard linguistics when he defines the work of the Holy Spirit, not as the crossing over from the signifier to what is signified (or from Scripture to the Word), but as the transformation of the signified into truth (p. 187). His thoroughly developed argument here about the signifiers, the signified, and the signification (pp. 187-92) is unique for Ellul.[1] In contrast to the main ideas in the other articles of this book, the linguistic elaborations of this discussion, to my knowledge, are repeated in no other major work. Only one of the disproved components, the notion that biblical thought was mythic in contrast to modern thought which is rational (pp. 182-83), is discussed at greater length in The New Demons (1973/73).

Ellul's emphases that the revelation does not vary essentially over time if God is God, that one cannot understand anything unless one receives and believes "the Revealed [One]" (p. 192), and that the decisive question is that of faith, which perceives a true signification (pp. 192-93), lead to his protest against any dilution of the situation of human beings before God. Ellul values hermeneutical tools for establishing the signification more exactly, but he recognizes that the more the rigor of hermeneutical methods grows, the more they lead to the evacuation of the vertical relation between God and human beings and to the negation of the possibility of signification (p. 194).

This grievance is expanded in a section of The Ethics of Freedom (1973, 1975/1976) that gives a full explication of Ellul's hermeneutical perspectives, without referring to the linguistic argument developed in this article. There Ellul objects to subordinating modern hermeneutics to the cultural background's fashions and fads, its scientism and tech-

---

1. One of my primary reasons for working to make these articles available in English was so that Ellul's hermeneutical arguments could be more widely known, since they don't appear elsewhere in his corpus.

nological ideology. On the opposite side, he also rejects biblical literalism. Instead, he stresses the necessary commitment to work to the utmost of our power, using many hermeneutical methods, in order that "there may be the unveiling of sense which can come only by the act of the Holy Spirit" (p. 163 of *Ethics of Freedom*). He offers as criteria for methods of exegesis, criticism, and analysis that they be oriented to the glory of God and the love of the neighbor (the same two qualifications that Ellul observed for freedom in the article of Chapter 5 of this book). By the former he means that our work is to bring out the splendor of God, for the text can only feebly transmit his revelation. The latter warns us that our critical freedom must never crush others by causing a scandal or destroying genuine faith. Ellul declares that this is the crux, in that the reasons for studying a biblical text are for better comprehension and adoration and for positive ministry to build up others. We know its value, therefore, not by the standard of the scientific method, but by its results in the hearts of people.

The "innocent notes" blame the hermeneutical problems on our society's crisis of language (pp. 195-96), a topic that Ellul elaborated in a set of books and articles, some of which had already appeared before this essay. His study of *Propaganda: The Formation of Men's Attitudes* (1962/65) had explored its pervasiveness in modern society, and *A Critique of the New Commonplaces* (1966/68) had examined the influence of unquestioned platitudes on contemporary thinking. These themes are probed further in *The Humiliation of the Word* (1981/85), Ellul's investigation of the growing predominance of the visual over the cognitive.

Ellul's call for intellectual humility — based on his suggestion that perhaps those who object so strenuously to words about Revelation, faith, or God do so because those truths are threatening to their system (p. 197) — is amplified in his section on "research" in *The Ethics of Freedom*. There he hypothesizes that our questioning of the Bible might be to avoid the questions that it puts to us. Being rooted in the Word and its questions, he insists, must be one of the prerequisites of research; another prerequisite is that this research must be located in the fellowship of the Church and must be guided by the confrontation of the community.

As Ellul concludes in "Innocent Notes," the signification received by faith challenges the crisis of language. Ultimately, either the biblical text carries the Revelation or it does not; it is a predecision of faith or of unbelief. Secular hermeneutics cannot give us "the central object, the goal, the real content, the hidden sense, or the life-giving spark of a text." Therefore, there must be a specific biblical hermeneutics, of which faith is the condition of existence and for which the biblical text itself gives the method (pp. 198-99).

All Ellul's biblical books are built on this understanding, which caused Ronald Ray of northern Nigeria, in an extended review of Ellul's "Notes," to praise him that his "exegetical labor" (to use a phrase from Ellul himself) has been so spiritually fruitful to so many. Ray calls Ellul "a disturbing thinker" because "he relentlessly insists that professionalism must not be allowed to efface biblical convictions concerning the nature and purpose of the Christian life," but he also observes that "certain reputable *biblical scholars* — Stuhlmacher and Childs in particular — are now saying things that are identical with what Ellul and Barth said all along." Certainly, "Barth and Ellul can now hardly be dismissed by biblical scholars as old-fashioned or passé."[2]

As the contemporary culture moves increasingly toward postmodernism, most scholars are recognizing the obsolescence of the methods Ellul decried in this article. How fascinating it is that thirty years ago Ellul called for a foundation in hermeneutics similar to that invited by current scholars. For example, consider the epistemological revisions required by the missiological appeal of Lesslie Newbigin (who bases his work on the insights of sociologist Michael Polanyi). Craig Van Gelder summarizes these three essential aspects necessary for a narrative approach to Scripture:

> (1) it is a product of a believing community who shared a common language, (2) there is a shared tradition into which new adherents are incorporated, and (3) certain faith commitments are necessary to understand its meaning.

As Van Gelder stresses,

> Enlightenment assumptions moved in the opposite direction on all three of these points, but it is becoming increasingly clear that such

2. Ronald R. Ray, "Jacques Ellul's Innocent Notes on Hermeneutics," *Interpretation* 33, 3 (July 1979): 271-72 and 263.

epistemological requirements shape the character of all human knowl-edge.[3]

Ellul's entire corpus shows the results of his similar understanding of the way to read the Bible — contrary to the hermeneutical modes of his time.

In the introduction of this chapter we glanced at Ellul's description of his own method in one of his biblical books. Let us close by observing his presuppositions in two of his ethical books. *To Will and to Do*, for example, begins with this announcement from Ellul:

> Lay the cards on the table. . . . I . . . confess that in this study and this research the criterion of my thought is the biblical revelation, the content of my thought is the biblical revelation, the point of departure is supplied by the biblical revelation, the method is the dialectic in accordance with which the biblical revelation is given to us, and the purpose is a search for the significance of the biblical revelation con-cerning ethics.[4]

Similarly, in *The Ethics of Freedom,* Ellul declares,

> As to my own ideological and philosophical presuppositions, I have tried incessantly for the past thirty years to clarify and criticize them in the light of revelation rather than using them to offer my own version of revelation.[5]

Though it has led to some glaring weaknesses in the particulars of Ellul's work, such single-minded devotion to the Revelation of God is his greatest strength in his massive interdisciplinary efforts. Would that we all were so faithful!

---

3. Craig Van Gelder, "Defining the Center — Finding the Boundaries: The Challenge of Re-Visioning the Church in North America for the Twenty-First Cen-tury," in *The Church Between Gospel and Culture: The Emerging Mission in North America,* ed. George R. Hunsberger and Craig Van Gelder (Grand Rapids: William B. Eerdmans, 1996), p. 35.

4. Jacques Ellul, *To Will and to Do: An Ethical Research for Christians,* trans. C. Edward Hopkin (Philadelphia: Pilgrim Press, 1969), p. 1.

5. Jacques Ellul, *The Ethics of Freedom,* trans. and ed. Geoffrey W. Bromiley (Grand Rapids: William B. Eerdmans, 1976), p. 8.

Works Cited

Works by Jacques Ellul

"Actualite de la Réforme." *Foi et Vie* 58, 2 (March/April 1959): 39-64.

Anarchy and Christianity. Trans. Geoffrey W. Bromiley. Grand Rapids: William B. Eerdmans, 1991.

Apocalypse: The Book of Revelation. Trans. George W. Schreiner. New York: Seabury Press, 1977.

"L'Argent." *Etudes Théologiques et Religieuses* 27, 4 (1952): 29-66.

Autopsy of Revolution. Trans. Patricia Wolf. New York: Alfred A. Knopf, 1971.

The Betrayal of the West. Trans. Matthew J. O'Connell. New York: Seabury Press, 1978.

"Chronique des Problèmes de Civilisation I: En Guise d'Avertissement." *Foi et Vie* 44, 6 (September/October 1946): 678-87.

A Critique of the New Commonplaces. Trans. Helen Weaver. New York: Alfred A. Knopf, 1968.

"Ellul's Response to the Symposium in His Honor at the University of Bordeaux, November 1993." Trans. Achim Koddermann and Carl Mitcham. *The Ellul Forum* 13 (July 1994): 18.

L'Empire du Non-Sens: L'Art et la Société Technicienne. Paris: Presses Universitaires de France, 1980.

"L'Empire du sens, pour moi, c'est la Bible." *France Catholique-Ecclesia* 1737 (28 March 1980): 10-11.

The Ethics of Freedom. Trans. Geoffrey W. Bromiley. Grand Rapids: William B. Eerdmans, 1976.

False Presence of the Kingdom. Trans. C. Edward Hopkin. New York: Seabury Press, 1972.

"Foi Chrétienne et Realité Sociale." *Free University Quarterly* 7, 2 (August 1960): 166-77.

Hope in Time of Abandonment. Trans. C. Edward Hopkin. New York: Seabury Press, 1973.

"How I Discovered Hope." Trans. Alfred Krass and Martine Wessel. *The Other Side* whole no. 102 (March 1980): 28-31.

The Humiliation of the Word. Trans. Joyce Main Hanks. Grand Rapids: William B. Eerdmans, 1985.

In Season, Out of Season: An Introduction to the Thought of Jacques Ellul. Based on interviews with Madeleine Garrigou-Lagrange. Trans. Lani K. Niles. San Francisco: Harper & Row, 1982.

Jesus and Marx: From Gospel to Ideology. Trans. Joyce Main Hanks. Grand Rapids: William B. Eerdmans, 1988.

The Judgment of Jonah. Trans. Geoffrey W. Bromiley. Grand Rapids: William B. Eerdmans, 1971.

Living Faith: Belief and Doubt in a Perilous World. Trans. Peter Heinegg. San Francisco: Harper & Row, 1980.

The Meaning of the City. Trans. Dennis Pardee. Grand Rapids: William B. Eerdmans, 1970.

Métamorphose du Bourgeois. Paris: Calmann-Levy, 1967.

Money and Power. Trans. LaVonne Neff. Downers Grove, IL: InterVarsity Press, 1984.

The New Demons. Trans. C. Edward Hopkin. New York: Seabury Press, 1975.

"Notes Innocentes Sur la 'Question Herméneutique.'" In *L'Evangile, Hier et Aujourd'hui: Melanges Offerts au Professeur Franz J. Leenhardt,* pp. 181-90. Genève: Editions Labor et Fides, 1968.

Perspectives on Our Age: Jacques Ellul Speaks on His Life and Work. Ed. William H. Vanderburg. Trans. Joachim Neugroschel. New York: Seabury Press, 1981.

The Political Illusion. Trans. Konrad Kellen. New York: Alfred A. Knopf, 1967.

The Politics of God and the Politics of Man. Trans. Geoffrey W. Bromiley. Grand Rapids: William B. Eerdmans, 1972.

Prayer and Modern Man. Trans. C. Edward Hopkin. New York: Seabury Press, 1970.

The Presence of the Kingdom. Trans. Olive Wyon. New York: Seabury Press, 1967. [2nd edition, Colorado Springs: Helmers & Howard, 1989.]

"Problèmes de Civilisation II: On Demande un Nouveau Karl Marx." *Foi et Vie* 45, 3 (May/June 1947): 360-74.

"Problèmes de Civilisation III: Le Realisme Politique." *Foi et Vie* 45, 7 (November/December 1947): 698-734.

Propaganda: The Formation of Men's Attitudes. Trans. Konrad Kellen and Jean Lerner. New York: Alfred A. Knopf, 1965.

Reason for Being: A Meditation on Ecclesiastes. Trans. Joyce Main Hanks. Grand Rapids: William B. Eerdmans, 1990.

"The Relationship Between Man and Creation in the Bible." Trans. W. Deller and Katharine Temple. In *Theology and Technology: Essays in Christian Analysis and Exegesis,* pp. 139-55. Ed. Carl Mitcham and Jim Grote. Lanham, MD: University Press of America, 1984.

"Le Sens de la Liberty chez Saint Paul." *Foi et Vie* 61, 3 (May/June 1962): 3-20.

"Signification actuelle de la Reforme." In *Protestantisme français,* pp. 137-165. Ed. Marc Boegner and André Siegfried. Paris: Plon, 1945.

The Subversion of Christianity. Trans. Geoffrey W. Bromiley. Grand Rapids: William B. Eerdmans, 1986.

"Sur le Pessimisme Chrétien." *Foi et Vie* 52, 2 (March/April 1954): 164-80.

"Technique and the Opening Chapters of Genesis." Trans. Greta Lindstrom and Katharine Temple. In *Theology and Technology: Essays in Christian Analysis and Exegesis,* pp. 123-37. Ed. Carl Mitcham and Jim Grote. Lanham, MD: University Press of America, 1984.

"Technique et Civilisation." *Free University Quarterly* 7, 2 (August 1960): 72-84.

The Technological Bluff. Trans. Joyce Main Hanks. Grand Rapids: William B. Eerdmans, 1990.

The Technological Society. Trans. John Wilkinson. New York: Vintage Books, 1964.

The Technological System. Trans. Joachim Neugroschel. New York: Continuum, 1980.

The Theological Foundation of Law. Trans. Marguerite Wieser. Garden City, NY: Doubleday, 1960.

To Will and To Do: An Ethical Research for Christians. Trans. C. Edward Hopkin. Philadelphia: Pilgrim Press, 1969.

Violence: Reflections from a Christian Perspective. Trans. Cecelia Gaul Kings. New York: Seabury Press, 1969.

What I Believe. Trans. Geoffrey W. Bromiley. Grand Rapids: William B. Eerdmans, 1988.

"Work and Calling." Trans. James S. Albritton. In *Callings!* pp. 18-44. Ed. James Y. Holloway and Will D. Campbell. New York: Paulist Press, 1974.

Other Works Cited

Bradley, Bill. *Time Present, Time Past: A Memoir.* New York: Alfred A. Knopf, 1996.

Calvin, John. *Letters, Compiled from the Original Manuscripts and Edited with Historical Notes.* 4 volumes. Ed. Jules Bonnet. Trans. M. R. Gilchrist and David Constable. 1858; repr. New York: Burt Franklin, 1973.

Dawn, Marva J. "The Concept of 'The Principalities and Powers' in the Works of Jacques Ellul." Ph.D. dissertation, University of Notre Dame, 1992.

Gill, David. "My Journey with Ellul." *The Ellul Forum* 13 (1994): 8-9.

Hanks, Joyce Main. "Jacques Ellul, 1912-1994." *The Ellul Forum* 13 (1994): 4.

————, compiler, with the assistance of Rolf Asal. "Jacques Ellul: A Comprehensive Bibliography." In *Research in Philosophy and Technology.* London: Jai Press, 1984.

Illich, Ivan. "An Address to 'Master Jacques.'" *The Ellul Forum* 13 (July 1994): 16-17.

Neville, David. "Confronted with New Perspectives: Reading Jacques Ellul." *Faith and Freedom* 3, 4 (December 1994): 25.

O'Connor, Flannery. *Mystery and Manners.* Ed. Sally Fitzgerald and Robert Fitzgerald. New York: Farrar, Straus & Giroux, 1961.

Postman, Neil. *Amusing Ourselves to Death: Public Discourse in the Age of Show Business.* New York: Viking Penguin, 1985.

————. *Technopoly: The Surrender of Culture to Technology.* New York: Alfred A. Knopf, 1992.

WORKS CITED

Sass, Louis A. *Madness and Modernism: Insanity in the Light of Modern Art, Literature, and Thought.* New York: Basic Books, 1992.

Van Gelder, Craig. "Defining the Center — Finding the Boundaries: The Challenge of Re-Visioning the Church in North America for the Twenty-First Century." In *The Church Between Gospel and Culture: The Emerging Mission in North America,* pp. 26-51. Ed. George R. Hunsberger and Craig Van Gelder. Grand Rapids: William B. Eerdmans, 1996.